BECOMING CANCER FREE

NATHAN CRANE

Testimonials

"I was diagnosed with pancreatic cancer, and you and the great work you do are one extremely strong reason that I have complete faith that I will make a complete recovery. Into a world of grim statistics, you bring light, hope and the power of knowledge and truth. Empowering is the descriptor that keeps coming to mind. As you know, It makes all the difference to mindset and survival. How can I ever thank you for that? I thought Becoming Cancer-Free was the latest chapter in empowering the patient and fueling the will to live. What I found especially helpful were the suggestions you had to make each step actionable and achievable. Please keep up the great work. It's lifeblood to a cancer patient. With great appreciation and kind regards" —
Frank F.

"This information is very convincing and gives a lot of hope. Your clear instructions give a lot of support. This is what I admired the most and inspired me the most. I highly recommend the book to others." — **Brigitte H**.

"I found this book extremely helpful. I am over a year out from my cancer diagnosis (stage 3A breast cancer) and the topics covered were the fuel I needed to keep my momentum going with my care." —**Cameesha G.**

"I have been diagnosed with metastatic breast cancer. It has always seemed counterintuitive to me to use treatments that I knew would cause harm. I cannot begin to tell you how much I appreciate what you are doing. I'm very excited and encouraged by your information and systems and am entirely committed to following through. Thank you very much." — **Debbie V.**

"Dear Nathan, I thoroughly enjoyed your Becoming Cancer Free book. My favorite chapters were the ones that dealt with nutrition and cancer and stress and cancer, and I especially loved the information about the people who survived cancer. Thank you for what you are doing to help cancer patients. Sincerely," — **Lynn P.**

Acknowledgements

Sometimes in life devastating experiences outside of our control sweep through like a tornado destroying parts of ourselves and our family. One of those experiences was losing my Grandfather to cancer in 2013. I had no idea how his death would impact me and the work I would come to do in the world. This book is the culmination of nearly a decade of my life focused on learning and researching cancer, its causes and its solutions. After hundreds of interviews with Doctors, Scientists, and Survivors, I discovered there are real solutions to cancer that most Medical Doctors, let alone the average person, have no idea about. On the other side of darkness, ignorance and devastation, is possibility, light, and awakening. I want to thank my Mother for her ongoing love throughout my life, my Father for his continuous support, my wife for being by my side, my children for teaching me how to be a better human being, my assistant director Ella for helping with this project and my designer Jet for the technical side of pulling this book together. I want to thank my past failures and broken partnerships for teaching me patience, commitment and forgiveness, and I want to thank all of my community members and readers who share with me how this work has helped change and transform their lives for the better - I couldn't do any of this work without all of you, so thank you!

With love and appreciation,

Nathan

Table of Contents

Chapter 1

The Foundations

Welcome to Becoming Cancer-Free, 7 Simple, Effective and Proven Steps to Take Back Control of Your Health - This is a 7-step system where you will learn scientifically validated methods and strategies I've learned over the past 15 years from hundreds of world leading cancer experts and cancer conquerors to help you embody a cancer free lifestyle.

I'm truly honored that you're here with me, and I promise that our time together will be valuable and effective. This 7-step system is designed to help you navigate the complexity of cancer and all of the causes, physiological functions, scientific research, and healing modalities that can accelerate your healing, in the most simple and easy to follow blueprint I can make possible.

I know this is a huge promise, and I truly appreciate the value of your time, as well as your commitment to spend time together with me over these coming chapters to truly help you take back control of your health.

And let's be clear, I'm not promising that by going through this book, you're guaranteed to reverse cancer. I think we both know that's a promise nobody can make, not even the best oncologists in the world.

But what I am promising is that by the time we're done with this book, you will be exponentially more informed, educated, inspired, and equipped to make effective changes that can transform your life forever - with the ultimate goal of being to add years to your life, and more life to those years.

And hey, if in the process, you are able to completely reverse cancer just like Elaine Gibson, Chris Wark, and Dr. Veronique DeSaulniers, all of whom I've spent a lot of time interviewing them and learning from them over the years on how they were able to reverse multiple forms of cancer, and even stage 4 cancer, then it's an added bonus and something we will celebrate together!

The truth is, for most people, cancer is incredibly scary. They are afraid of it being a death sentence, they're told they have 6 months, or 1 year, or 2 years left to live, or they're told that without surgery or chemotherapy or radiation their odds of surviving are slim to none.

But I'm here to tell you that those scary prognostic methods are not for your well-being, and they're not based on all the facts either. As Dr. Francisco Contreras, MD says in my award-winning documentary film titled "Cancer; The Integrative Perspective," he says, "we're taught in medical school to give the worst case scenario as the prognosis, to prevent us from being sued."

Think about that for a moment. They're not taught to inspire you, give you hope, teach you all of your alternative options, some of which are more effective than conventional medicine as proven by science - they're taught to give you the worst case scenario, so if and when you die, nobody can sue them. It's crazy, but it's the world we currently live in.

Medical doctors might have good hearts, and good intentions, and even some great equipment for treating acute traumas like ruptured organs, gunshot wounds, or severed limbs, but when it comes to chronic diseases, it's well known in the holistic health field and very well understood scientifically that medical doctors simply are not trained in treating chronic diseases like cancer.

As Dr. Leigh Erin Connealy, who is an integrative MD told me when filming her for my documentary, she said, "we're taught in medical school how to diagnose, how to do surgery, and pharmacology, how to prescribe drugs, and yet, we're only taught a few hours of nutrition"

Even though there are thousands of peer-reviewed studies in the scientific literature discussing the impact of diet, environment and lifestyle on cancer and other metabolically related diseases like heart disease and diabetes, most conventional medical doctors and oncologists are unfortunately not trained more than a few hours in nutrition and lifestyle. And the nutritional training they have, is primarily in things that are already cured such as Vitamin C for scurvy.

As of this writing I've personally spent over 15 years studying, researching, learning about and experimenting with natural health. I've invested thousands of hours, not 4 hours, literally thousands, researching, experimenting, and interviewing hundreds of experts in nutrition, health and healing, neuroscience, quantum physics, cellular rejuvenation, the science of exercise, spirituality, epigenetics, and personal transformation - and I can tell you, I still don't have all the answers - but I do have foundations, principles and strategies that can help you take back control of your health - and the truth is, what we're going to discover together during this book goes way beyond what our medical doctors have been taught up until this point.

As Thomas Edison once stated, "The doctor of the future will give no medication but will interest his patients in the care of the human frame, diet and in the cause and prevention of disease."

Unfortunately, medical doctors have not been taught the cause and prevention, or even reversal of diseases. They are great at diagnosing disease, treating acute traumas, utilizing some life-saving antibiotics like penicillin, and prescribing medications that mask symptoms.

The good news is that there are more and more Doctors every day being trained in disciplines like functional medicine where they learn about nutrition and lifestyle for health and healing.

Even so, most Doctors today are still primarily prescribing drugs as their go-to solution for disease. We all know what happens when someone is prescribed medication, especially when you're told it has devastating side effects. One drug turns into two, two drugs turn into four, and before you know it you're downing a handful of pills three times a day every day for the rest of your life, dealing with a whole host of uncomfortable and painful symptoms, which are often worse than the original symptoms you had to begin with, or in many cases with most stages of cancer, no original symptoms at all.

And even antibiotics get heavily overused, causing damage to the healthy microflora in your intestines, harming your immune system, when other natural solutions like garlic, onion, high dose vitamin C, Vitamin D, cayenne, zinc, echinacea, prebiotics, and probiotics together can do a better job, not only helping eliminate the bacteria or virus, but also help build the immune system without damaging healthy cells.

But please understand, this is not about bashing on medical doctors. If I were in a car crash, had a severed limb, or ruptured an organ, believe me!... I would be in the ER as quick as anyone. But when it comes to health and healing, especially chronic health challenges like cancer, and I'm saying most, not all, most medical doctors don't have the tools needed to actually help prevent or reverse that disease.

And that's true with bacterial and viral infections as well. Antibiotics and prescription drugs may help kill the pathogens, but they don't do anything to help support the most powerful resource in your body that has the potential to eliminate just about every infection, as well as reverse and eliminate metabolic diseases like cancer.

With that said, there are a number of very effective and incredibly knowledgeable medical doctors who realized at some point in their careers, that the form of medicine they were practicing was not actually helping people heal.

They realized, through some miracle of grace, that the profession they so dearly loved, was run by pharmaceutical companies, and they weren't actually helping people heal from diseases like cancer, diabetes, and autoimmunity. They somehow stumbled upon research, or some eye-opening case studies, or attended a conference or a summit or read a magazine or watched a documentary like the ones I've produced over the years, and it began to open their eyes and send them down the path of intense research into natural, holistic and integrative medicine.

They discovered that through a more holistic approach, they could actually help their patients not only understand the true causes of their disease, and eliminate those causes from their lives, but also go beyond the symptoms of the disease to improve the true healing capacity of the human body, and get extraordinary results.

Many of them completely changed their approach in their practices, and began guiding their patients through the most effective cancer-fighting diets and exercise, utilizing high dose nutritional therapeutics, dealing with and healing the underlying emotional trauma and neurological conditions, and implementing immune-enhancing practices that help the body to fully heal itself.

They started seeing miraculous results, patients stopping the growth of cancer in their bodies, and in many cases, reversing it completely, while using non-toxic medicine, not only extending the length of their lives, but improving the quality of their lives exponentially.

These are the doctors I have actively been seeking out since 2013 and interviewing them, researching their methods, visiting their clinics, studying their patients, and learning everything I possibly could about the true causes of cancer, the most effective cancer treatments, and what each of us can do to prevent and reverse cancer, so we no longer have to be afraid of it.

So why am I so passionate about helping people prevent and reverse cancer, especially since I haven't gone through cancer myself - well in 2013, after visiting my Grandpa in Southern Arizona, watching him suffer in tremendous pain, not from the cancer, but from the treatments of chemotherapy and radiation, and then pass away shortly after that, I knew there had to be a better way.

I felt so bad watching him suffer like that, and not being able to do anything to help. Having been heavily involved in studying and experimenting with natural health, personal development and spiritual traditions since 2005, I thought at that point I knew a lot about health and should have been able to help him.

But I realized when seeing my Grandpa go through that pain and suffering, that I actually didn't know much about cancer specifically. I felt afraid and helpless like most people when it comes to cancer. I remember talking to him about fruits and vegetables, and him saying that his Doctor told him he couldn't eat the foods that could actually help him because his immune system was destroyed from the chemical treatments and the bacteria on the vegetables could kill him - which to me made literally no sense at the time. And after I went back home with my wife and daughter, I decided I would never be in that position again.

I decided I would do everything I possibly could to learn from people who have overcome cancer, who are treating cancer patients successfully, and who understand the deeper causes and solutions to cancer, so I, my family, or anyone else I come into contact with, would never have to be afraid or helpless again.

What I've discovered, and what you'll discover over the coming chapters, is that cancer is a wake-up call. It's an opportunity to re-evaluate your life from a new perspective, and decide if the life you have been living is the life you want to continue living, or if you're ready to step up to a higher quality, happier, healthier more fulfilling life that you truly deserve.

What I've discovered is that everyone is capable of truly incredible things. And that's not just some raw personal growth statement - Watching people go from nothing, from homeless, from near-death, from given only a month to live, to not only reversing their cancer completely, but living decades past their so-called expiration date and turning their life into something of incredibly meaning and value to themselves and others - I know with all my heart that everyone, including you, is capable of living a truly extraordinary life, and everyone is capable of overcoming any disease. Even stage-4 cancers, and beyond.

Take Elaine Gibson for example. A woman who I've known for quite a few years. Elaine is a Grandmother now in her seventies, a lecturer, author, teacher and 2-time cancer survivor. The first time she reversed cancer in 2001, which was only at stage 1, she used a combination of IPT and a complete diet and lifestyle change.

When I interviewed her again recently for my Global Cancer Symposium 2.0, she shared with me that when cancer came back the second time, about 7 years later, it was stage 4 Non-Hodgkin's Lymphoma, and she was not only shocked as you can imagine, but the doctor told her she would not see her grandchildren grow up. What a horrible thing to say to someone, right?!

Thank God she didn't take that prognosis as a fact, and over ten years later, in the year 2020, I'm able to interview her not only healthier than she's ever been at 75 years young, but completely cancer-free.

What you'll learn is that Elaine looked at her second cancer diagnosis as a wake-up call and an opportunity to learn more about the deeper causes of the disease and make more lifestyle changes that eventually led her to completely reversing stage 4 cancer - and one of the most important things she changed and learned to help her reverse cancer a second time, I'm going to share with you in depth in step 3 of this book.

And what's interesting is that through more testing, Elaine found out she "had a gene out of whack", and by using an integrative approach, using the most effective diet, lifestyle and holistic methods that you're going to learn during this book, and finding a single pharmaceutical to combine with her natural approach, she not only reharmonized her gene, but completely reversed stage 4 cancer, and is still cancer-free as she's teaching and helping others find hope and healing through their journeys.

And if you see Elaine, you'd agree with me, that she looks like she's 55 years old, and has the energy and youthfulness of a much younger person, and at 75 years old, she's got so much more to give. Clearly what she's done with her health and her life over the past 20 years has been working! And you're going to learn over the coming chapters exactly what she, and many others have done, and are doing every day to prevent and reverse cancer using effective, natural, and integrative approaches.

If you're wondering whether cancer can truly be fully understood, and even reversed in just 7 steps, then you're not alone. I'm here to tell you that cancer has been made so complicated, and is so misconstrued, for one main reason. It's a multi-billion-dollar business. In 2019, the cancer drug market alone reached over $167,000,000,000 increasing at nearly 10% annually since 2015.

Do those drugs actually cure cancer? In most cases, the answer is no. Chemotherapy for example, being one of the most prescribed treatments from an oncologist today, in addition to radiation and surgery, has had the largest study ever done on a 5-year survival rate using chemotherapy across 22 major adult malignancies, which studied over 72,000 cancer patients in Australia and more than 150,000 cancer patients in the USA, and the average 5-year survival rate using chemotherapy was… Take a guess - 65% of people lived past 5 years using chemotherapy? Too high? What about 45%? That seems realistic for a multi hundred-billion-dollar industry that is prescribing chemotherapy to most cancer patients? Still too high? What about 35%? I mean, if it's less than 35%, what are we doing here?!

Here's the truth, the 5-year total average survival rate using chemotherapy on the 22 major cancers are 2.3% in Australia, and a whopping 2.1% in the USA.

Take that in for a moment. That's nearly a 98% failure rate, with a multi-billion-dollar drug industry.

Can you guess the highest rate of survival with chemotherapy? It was testicular cancer, coming in at over 40%. What do you think was the lowest rate? How many cancers came in at 0 survivors? 9! 9 forms of cancer came in at 0 survivors using chemotherapy! That includes prostate cancer, kidney cancer, bladder cancer, uterine cancer, and more!

With a 2.1% effective rate, that means chemotherapy, across most cancers, has nearly a 98% failure rate. If your doctor told you that their treatment was 98% likely to fail, would you do it?

Probably not! But they prescribe this treatment every single day. How often? In the USA alone, over 650,000 people are prescribed chemotherapy every year! Not only does chemotherapy not work for most cancers, but it destroys the immune system, making it harder to combat infections that often lead to death.

Now, here's the kicker, being a cancer-survivor, from the medical term, doesn't mean that you overcome cancer. So let's say for example, some cancers have a 40% survival rate using a combination of radiation and chemotherapy.

Do you know what survival actually means when said by a medical doctor? It means that you live past 5 years after being diagnosed. And that doesn't matter if those years due to treatment were the worst years of your life, and it doesn't matter if you die on one day after 5 years - you are still considered a cancer survivor.

If the treatments were actually effective, they wouldn't need to set the bar so freaking low! A true cancer cure, or cancer survivor, in my opinion, and from my definition, is someone who has cancer one day, and after whatever protocols they follow, they get their scans back, and they no longer have cancer.

That's the way it should be, right? But because the medical conventional therapies are so ineffective, remember, a 98% failure rate with majority of cancers using chemotherapy, they have to set their standard so low, and just like my Grandpa, who went from being failure active, but not very healthy, to being in so much pain and suffering from the chemo and radiation, to dying from it - that is the unfortunate truth for most people today.

And if they do miraculously live past 5 years from their diagnosis using conventional methods, the cancer either has not gone away, and continues to spread until it does become a real problem, or it comes back with a vengeance, as has happened to many people I've interviewed over the years.

So, please know, I'm not saying you shouldn't use conventional medicine. In fact, I'll actually tell you the opposite during this book. You SHOULD use conventional medicine. But only, and this is a big only - if you understand the true consequences of it, you know your true potential survival rate, and you do everything else I share with you over the coming chapters to strengthen your immune system and take back control of your health so your body has the best fighting chance at surviving.

But I don't want you to just survive. And if I were to make a guess, I'm guessing you don't only want to survive either, I'm guessing you're like me, and you want to thrive! You want to live a healthy, happy and meaningful life. You want to continue growing, learning, contributing, and enjoying life for years to come.

And that's exactly what this book is about. It's about helping you not only add years to your life, but to make your years ahead the best years yet! How is that possible you might ask? That's exactly what I'll share with you in Step 1, which is to Take Back Your Power!

Taking back your power is about accelerating your healer within. It's about self-responsibility, and self-empowerment. You'll discover that cancer doesn't have to be a death sentence, and that while there are many paths to healing, there are simple and proven foundations, that as long as you build upon these foundations, everything else that can be beneficial to your healing path will be supported by these foundational elements.

But you've got to get the foundations right. You've got to make sure your foundation is not only strong, but accurate. If you build a sky rise tower on top of sand, it's going to fall and crash pretty quickly.

But if you build a sky rise tower on top of cement, it's going to be strong, but if you've got the wrong blueprints, then you're going to end up with a leaning tower of Pizza! :-)

So in Steps 2-6 we're going to help you build a rock solid foundation so you can build your tower (your future) no matter how many years that is, on top of a strong solid surface so the higher you grow, the stronger, healthier and happier you'll become.

Cancer, once fully understood what it is, how it works, how and why our bodies make it, and what we can do to prevent cancer cells from growing and spreading, is actually a very simple thing. And that's my job, to make something so complex like cancer, a multi-billion dollar industry filled with unethical "nonprofit" organizations and cancer walks to "find the cure," most of whom are putting billions of dollars into drugs that do very little towards actually finding a cure, other than lining the pockets of pharmaceutical companies with billions and billions of dollars, my job, and my passion is to simplify all of the complexities into a formula of foundations and principles that anyone can follow.

So is it possible that cancer can be fully understood, and even reversed in only 7 steps? The short answer is Absolutely! And I'll prove it with hard science, anecdotal healing stories, and direct testimony from the leading minds in the fields of cancer over these coming chapters.

And before we dive into the 7 steps, there's something every cancer patient needs to come to terms with. And I need you to understand that this next part is coming from love, from integrity and humility, and from personal experience.

And that thing every cancer patient needs to come to term with, is death.

The reality is, one day, we're all going to die. I know, dark, right? But it's the truth. It's the truth we all have to accept if we're truly going to live. William Wallace, one of Scotland's greatest heroes who led the Scottish forces to successfully become free from England's tyrannical rule, once said, "Every man dies, but not every man really lives." And I would add to that, every woman dies and not every woman really lives.

Once we accept the fact that we're going to die, whether you believe in Heaven or Hell, or in reincarnation, or believe in nothing at all, the truth is, we're all here to die, but even more so, I believe we're all here to live. To truly live. To live with joy and happiness. To live with health and vitality. To enjoy the simple beauties in nature, and the laughs of our grandchildren. To contribute to society in a meaningful way, and to lie on our deathbeds, having learned from our mistakes, peacefully reflecting back on our lives saying to ourselves, "I truly am grateful for the life I lived. I have made the world a better place, if even only for my children, my grandchildren, or for my neighbors, or for those I don't even know, I know I contributed in some meaningful way."

As Hunter S Thompson so famously wrote, "Life should not be a journey to the grave with the intention of arriving safely in a pretty and well preserved body, but rather to skid in broadside in a cloud of smoke, thoroughly used up, totally worn out, and loudly proclaiming "Wow! What a Ride!"

I want to lie there in my death bed saying, "I squeezed out every ounce of life possible and enjoyed so much of it, helping guide others from the dark to the light, having loved and been loved, having appreciated and been appreciated, having learned and grown mentally, emotionally, physically and spiritually and contributed in some meaningful way to others."

I believe these want to be the thoughts of every dying person, knowing that the next life, the one beyond this one, will be just as good, if not better. Science tells us that energy never dies... and what are we made of? 100% energy. They say energy never dies, it only transforms.

While our bodies transform into food for microbes and compost for the soil, bringing new life to the life on earth, I truly believe our spirits transcend into another dimension, one that is free from the limitations we experience here on earth, and I truly believe all of our spirits transcend into a place that is free from pain and suffering.

Whatever you believe happens after this life, we need to come to terms with it, and remove the fear from our minds, and be appreciative and fulfilled in the life we lived here, letting go of our regrets, and enjoying the years we have left on this earth.

And if you cannot lie on your deathbed yet with those thoughts of deep gratitude and inner joy and fulfillment, then you still have work to do! And I believe we all still have work to do. I truly believe that you are still here on this earth for a reason, and whether you have 5 years left, or 50 years left, there's still so much more you can get from and give to this beautiful thing we call life.

Of course I cannot promise you that you will cure your cancer and live your best years yet, or that you will overcome your disease and live another 20 or more years like others have done.

But what I can promise you is that if you take to heart and really learn, and then fully commit and implement what you're going to learn through all 9 chapters of this book, that you will have a significantly higher chance of not only slowing your cancer growth, but potentially reversing it all together, and at the very least, discover a healthier, happier and more fulfilled side of yourself that you might have never experienced before, OR, have been missing for a long time.

As Dr. Thomas Lodi, a dear friend and colleague who is a world renowned holistic medical doctor with clinics from Arizona to Thailand, says, "when people come to me, they're not really asking how do I get rid of cancer, they're asking, how do I stop making cancer?"

And that's what you're going to learn. How to stop making cancer. And with the science that supports these methods, the action and discipline you implement moving forward, and a little bit of grace, we can catch your cancer in time, to not only add years to your life, but add more quality, joy and fulfillment to those years as well.

No matter where you're at in your healing journey, whether you're just starting down this path, or you've been at it for years, I promise that you will learn empowering methods and strategies that you can start implementing immediately to support you on your healing journey.

In step one you're going to learn a powerful technique that will help your mind begin taking back the power it's given away so it can direct your body to activate its own innate healing response.

Whether you decide to go through this entire book all at once, or own it so you can go through it again and again. Just know, every moment you delay your healing and delay making the changes necessary to support your healing, and every moment you waste living a life that is unfulfilling and unhappy, is a moment you can't get back.

But here's the good news, you don't have to rush into any treatment or healing protocol, you can take the time to truly learn what options you have, and get additional advice before making huge and potentially life altering decisions.

Cancer has been growing inside your body for years, and even if you're in late stages of cancer, your decision making process needs to be a bit more urgent, but you still have time to learn and make informed decisions for your health, because one wrong decision in your treatment protocols, such as surgery, radiation or chemotherapy, could literally mean long term health consequences, or even death, so before you choose big decisions like that, inform yourself of all of your options, and of all the consequences, both positive and negative, before deciding.

Spend the time really studying these chapters, consulting with the experts I recommend, and following through with your own research, reasoning and intuition as you move forward. So many people take one thing they hear as absolute fact, without digging deeper, or sitting quietly and listening to that inner voice. Your inner voice, when coming from a place of calmness, and certainty, can be one of the best guides in your life.

And if you've already gone down the path of conventional treatment, without success, and are ready to try a more natural, effective and integrative approach, then these foundations and principles and methods are exactly what are going to help you along your journey.

Over the coming chapters, I will not only share with you what is working, and what has been working in the advanced fields of neuroscience, integrative oncology, quantum physics, physiology, and botanical therapeutics, but I will share with you the step by step approach to living your healthiest, happiest, and most fulfilling life - even while having cancer.

So as one of my mentors, the late Jim Rohn used to say, "If you're ready say I'm ready!" Are you ready? If you're ready to take back control of your health, take serious action every day towards your healing journey, be fully committed to the process, take to heart everything you'll learn over the coming chapters, and follow through with the 7 step plan I will lay out for you, then you can take back control of your health, and I'm here to guide you along the way. So if you're ready, let's begin! It's time for step 1.

Chapter 2

Step 1. Take Back Your Power: Accelerate Your Healer Within

Are you ready to learn the 7 simple and effective steps for taking back control of your health? For empowering your mind and your body to activate its innate and incredible healing potential?

Well I'm excited for you! And I want to congratulate you! Most people who buy a book, or an online program, unfortunately never even get past the first couple of chapters or lessons. So, congratulations! The fact that you made it through my introduction, and you're here, means you're committed, and I truly honor and commend you for that! Now, all that's needed is to build your foundations with knowledge that will serve you, and then empower yourself to take daily action to make healing real in your life.

That's what step 1 is all about. It's about taking back your power so you can literally be em-powered to take control of your health. This is the foremost important step, which is why it's step #1.

Far too often we give our power over to others in white lab coats because we think they have all the answers. As you've discovered in my introduction, unfortunately most medical doctors don't have all the answers. In fact, they don't want all the answers. If they did, they would be open to hearing your healing stories outside of their care.

I recently spoke to someone who went to tell their medical doctor how they healed cancer using a natural approach. The doctor was shocked, and surprised when the patient came in for a checkup and their cancer was no longer visible on the scans. They thought it was a miracle! And when the patient says, "Doc let me tell you how I did it, I changed my diet, I exercised, I started meditating 2 hours a day...." the doctor rudely interrupted the patient and said, "never mind, it's just a miracle, it's unexplained, you don't need to tell me anymore, and that's all I need to know, congratulations you're cancer free - now get outta here!"

Now that's not true for all doctors, but it is a common theme from cancer survivors I've spoken to over the years who've healed themselves naturally, and their doctors simply don't want to know. If it's outside of the conventional model they were taught in med school, they chalk it up to luck, and miracles, rather than wanting to understand the science and foundations these people followed, knowingly or unknowingly, that led to their cancer going away.

Those are the foundations we're going to cover over the next 7 chapters. And the first foundation is to take back control of your own healing power. Take back control of your health. And there's 3 principles that make up this foundation.

Principle #1 is to become your own healer. What does that mean? Do you have to go to the Amazon to learn from shamans using psychedelics to connect to your inner healing powers? While that might be a path for some, it is not the path for most.

Becoming your own inner healer means recognizing that your body is perfectly designed and fully capable of healing itself. Your body was brilliantly designed, through some miraculous form, whether you believe in the big bang or God, there's no denying that the human body is one of the most incredible, sophisticated, wonderful things in the Universe.

Your body is estimated to have over 30 trillion cells, (yes that's Trillion with a T) and these cells are designed to all work in harmony with one another, duplicating, growing, dividing, dying, rebirthing so on and so forth, 24/7, while you sleep, eat, work and breath every single day for your entire life.

And not only are you made of human cells, but you're made of more bacterial and viral genes than you are human genes! Can you imagine? You have more bacteria and viruses inside your body than you do human.

It's also estimated that your body sends 11 million bits of information, every second, to your brain for processing. The best estimate of how many bits per second your conscious mind can process at a time, 50! Yep, that's right, a whopping 50 bits per second for you to consciously process what's going on around you. That means your body and brain are processing 99.999999% of everything you experience as a human being, automatically, without your conscious mind involved.

Now is that an incredibly intelligent design? Absolutely! Your body also has incredible mechanisms like the lymphatic system that removes dead cells and abnormal cells and cancer cells from your body. Your immune system helps to fight off invading pathogens, bacteria and viruses, as well as eliminate cancer cells. Your cardiovascular system helps to send nutrients through the bloodstream to the parts of your body that need it for healing and rejuvenation. Your nervous system helps to determine if something is safe or dangerous, and activates the fight or flight response, or the healing response.

All of these incredibly intelligent systems are working around the clock, 24/7, 365 days a year for one main reason... To help you live, to help you breath, to help you rejuvenate, to help you survive, and to help you thrive.

So when we talk about taking back control of your health, it's recognizing that while there are important coaches, leaders, doctors, and support teams to have in your corner supporting you on your path just like we'll talk about in step 2, at the end of the day, your body is perfectly equipped to fully heal itself.

All you have to do is understand the mechanisms that both trigger disease, (steps 3 and 4 of this book) and the mechanisms that create healing and rejuvenation (steps 3, 5, 6, and 7), and then take daily action to remove the causes of disease while implementing the methods that lead to true health.

When you take back the power for your own health, it means that you accept your responsibility to be a healer and to allow your body to heal itself. That doesn't mean you don't utilize the tools available to you or the good advice of other experts, it means that you understand that to create true healing, it requires creating an environment in your body and in your life that allows your body to do what it was designed to do - rejuvenate itself, and thrive!

Principle #2 is to be patient. I know, it sounds simple, and it should. This entire journey is simple, but that doesn't always mean it's easy, right? We've all heard the saying, "patience is a virtue." That was usually said by a school teacher or a parent who was teaching us that we can't get everything we want immediately like the new fancy bicycle or the superhero toy or latest doll or action figure that we wanted.

But there is tremendous wisdom in that single statement. Patience is a virtue. The definition of virtue means the quality of being virtuous or morally good. It also can mean excellence. In this case, both definitions apply. Being morally good means a lesson of what is right or prudent, or a person's standards of behavior or beliefs concerning what is and is not acceptable for them to do.

And the virtue of patience, or the lesson of what is right or prudent about patience, is that cancer, in most cases, usually takes 7 years or longer before it is identified - and in many cases, cancer has been growing in your body for decades before you ever knew it was there.

Was the cancer being patient? Absolutely! It slowly began growing and spreading, based on the environment it was given that supported its growth. Why did it take so long to become identified? The first reason is that to be caught on an MRI, which is usually done by accident, or during a routine checkup because someone either got hurt, or had some pain or some slight symptoms and the doctor couldn't figure out the cause, so he/she recommends an MRI, and by that time, the cancer has often spread to the lymph nodes, and if it's a tumor it's between 2cm-5cm in size, and is often found at stage 2 or later.

The second reason why cancer is usually not found until it's already been forming in your body for many years is because most cancers, until the very late stages, don't have any symptoms. That's right, you probably didn't know, but you can live with cancer for decades, in many cases, with very few symptoms, or even symptom free. That can both be a blessing, and a curse. The blessing is that you can be walking around with cancer for decades, and not know it, enjoying life and living normally.

The problem comes when it enters late stages, metastasizes to the rest of your body, and then your body starts to shut down and you die. For some people this could take years, for others, it can happen very quickly. It all depends on a lot of factors, but the #1 factor it depends on, is the environment in which the cancer cells live, which we'll dive deeply into in Step 4.

But, the important takeaway here is that cancer has been patiently growing, year after year, without you even knowing it. And our social conditioning is to immediately want to get rid of it. Our response is usually out of fear, and it's along the lines of wanting to get the cancer out of us as quickly as possible. Mostly because the doctor said, "you need to do surgery or chemotherapy or radiation immediately. Let's get you scheduled now. You only have 6 months left to live." They convince you to immediately set up an appointment out of fear, and usually sway you away from doing your own research, getting a second or 3rd opinion from experts in multiple health fields outside of conventional medicine, and rarely encourage you to consult with your higher power or use your intuition or your own reasoning - just do what they say right now, or you're going to die.

You see, that's giving your power over to someone else who believes they have all the answers for your health, even though you now understand they might have some of the answers, but they rarely have all of them.

And that's true for me. I don't have all of the answers for you. And you shouldn't believe everything I say. What I want you to do is listen, read, learn, experiment, and question everything I say, with an open mind, and do your own research, get your own answers, find your own solutions, and be committed to the learning and growing process.

The truth is, I will lay out the 15+ years of research and guidance I've discovered in interviewing and learning from the best minds in the health field for you to shorten your own learning journey, turning centuries of knowledge into hours of learning and growth, but I still encourage you to dig deeper, ask questions, and get multiple opinions...

...just be careful who you're getting your opinions from - are they from people who are actually in the field, hands on, researching, learning from the most successful, and helping people heal from cancer, or even healing themselves from cancer like all of the experts and cancer survivors I've studied since 2013? Or are they just another so-called social media health expert regurgitating something they saw on some website? Or are they just another run of the mill medical doctor who's only tool kit is surgery, drugs and radiation?

Remember in the introduction when I told you that a number of medical doctors I've interviewed have all told me the only nutritional training they had in all of their years of medical school was about 4 hours' worth? And that they are told not to research or even listen to anything to do with natural or holistic medicine? They are told that there's no science supporting it - which of course is all lies, and why are these lies perpetrated on good hearted caring med students who actually want to help people?

For one main reason we talked about, drugs are worth trillions of dollars, and the pharmaceutical companies control the medical literature that the doctors learn in school. This is not some far out conspiracy, it's a fact.

And remember when I told you that in 15 years of my own experience in the health field, I don't have 4 hours of nutritional and holistic health training and research and experimentation - I have thousands of hours, and much of it is dedicated to learning from the best minds in the field. And even so, with thousands of hours of training and research, I'm still learning more to do this day. But my job for you is to take all of that research and experience, and make it as simple and easy to understand and implement so you can get results quickly!

So please make sure where you're getting your information is from a reputable source, and from people who actually are doing the work, doing the research, seeing the case-studies, and learning from those who truly are seeing healing happen again and again.

So why do we have to be patient? Because healing takes time. Plain and simple. It took a long time to get sick, it's going to take time to heal. The good news is, while it usually takes 7 or more years for cancer to be found, and in some cases it's been forming for decades, it can often be slowed very quickly, and when full recovery does happen, it often happens in only a matter of a few short years.

Elaine Gibson, after receiving her stage 4 cancer diagnosis, "went to town" doing everything in her power to use natural and integrative approaches to healing herself, all of which you'll learn in the upcoming chapters, and received her clean bill of health back in 2012 after only about 4 years of dedication to her healing. And at the time of me recording this, she is 75 years young, and still going strong! Truly incredible. From decades of damage just a few short years, she's totally healed and happier, more energetic and fulfilling a beautiful life purpose, adding more years to her life and much more life to her years.

But the important thing to remember is that she didn't sit back and do nothing, she continued learning, implementing, and taking action every single day, realizing that it would take some time to heal, but being committed to the process, so she not only was patient, but she followed principle #3.

And **principle #3** is, never give up. Becoming your own healer is the first step to taking back your power. Being patient, yet taking action every day, is the second step. And the third most important step of taking back your power is to stay committed, stay focused, and never give up.

That doesn't mean that if something isn't working, that you don't change your approach. Actually the opposite is true. If something isn't working, and you're not seeing any progress whatsoever in a reasonable amount of time, then you might need to add something, or change something.

But first we have to define "reasonable amount of time" and we have to define "results." What is a reasonable amount of time for seeing progress with cancer? In my experience, and if it were me, I would dedicate to a holistic protocol for at least 6 months, and if there are not any positive results whatsoever, then I might need to add something else, or change something up. And if you're really committed, you might give it a year, or you might want to base it on less time, but I wouldn't base it on anything less than 6 months. You can usually see changes in your health in 6 months, and sometimes in only 3 months, but the reality is most people will not see changes that quickly, so being patient is absolutely paramount.

But just as important, we need to define what we mean by results. It's highly unlikely that if you have been growing cancer in your body for, let's say 15 years, that it's going to completely go away in just 6 months. Is it possible? Sure, anything is possible. Is it likely, the truth is, no. Just like Elaine, it will likely take years, in her case just over 4 years to reverse stage 4, and that's if you're doing everything right. But can it happen in less than 4 years, absolutely!

But in defining what "results" means, a positive result of progress is not only the reduction of the cancer itself, but both the slowing of the spread, or the stopping of the spread itself. For example, if you are doing a scan every 3-6 months, and the cancer has been spreading and growing at a certain rate, and then you start implementing a healing and holistic lifestyle, and the cancer spread slows, or stops completely, that is major progress! Just slowing the spread of cancer is a big result! Something to celebrate, and something to show you that you're on the right track!

And if you slow or stop the cancer enough to where you can continue enjoying life with more energy and more happiness, it can not only add years to your life, but add more quality and fulfillment to your life as well.

That's why you must never give up. Keep learning, keep growing mentally, emotionally and spiritually, keep implementing healing strategies, and do check-ups every 3-6 months to track your progress. For some people healing will happen quicker, for others it will take longer, but one thing is for certain, if you only commit for a few months, then go back to your lifestyle that caused cancer in the first place, you will not get the results you're looking for.

In step 4, we will cover how to remove and reduce all of the things in your life that directly cause cancer, and simply by removing these things, you will accelerate your healing journey exponentially, which can contribute to slowing the spread of cancer. Once you know what actually causes cancer, you can remove those causes, and your body will begin to harmonize back to its natural healing state, and then in steps 5 and 6 you will learn how to nourish your body, based in science, that actually causes cellular regeneration and cancer-cell elimination.

But let's not jump too far ahead, we still need to help you build your success team so you don't have to go alone, and can glean and learn from the decades of knowledge and experience that these experts have to support you on your healing journey.

So let's make these 3 principle of step #1 STICK before we move on. It's one thing to learn something, it's another to know it in your heart and in your body as truth. The way to knowing is through repetition, and embodiment. It's through practice.

So here's what I want you to do. Get a piece of paper or a sticky note, right now, and a pen or a marker, and let's do a little exercise to make this stick. Go ahead, I'll give you a couple of seconds…

Ok, you got it? Write these 3 statements on it. I call these the 3 declarations for taking back your power

1. I am becoming my own healer, I am responsible for my health (Again)

2. I will be patient, I know true healing takes time, knowledge, and action (Again)

3. I will never give up, I will persevere until I heal, learning, improving and growing as I go (Again)

Now, please do this with me right now. Raise your hand that you brush your teeth with. For me it's my right hand, which one do you brush with?

Good, now take your other hand, and place that opposite hand on your heart, and take a big deep breath into your heart - please, do this with me now -

Take a big deep breath into your heart, and begin to feel gratitude for something in your life.

Think of something you can feel deeply grateful for. Maybe you can feel grateful for your life and for the potential healthy future ahead.

Maybe you can feel grateful for the roof over your head, food in the fridge, and the life you still have.

Maybe you can feel grateful for family, or friends. Or something simple like a warm bed and a nice meal.

Feel grateful for something in your life right now. Feel it spread through your entire body. And now, with your hand still over heart, repeat with me:

1. I am my own healer, I am responsible for my health, I truly can heal from within

2. I will be patient, I know true healing takes time, knowledge, and daily action

3. I will never give up, I will persevere until I heal, learning, improving, enjoying and growing as I go

Now feel it, sense it, know it to be true, embody it into your physiology.

And now here's your first assignment. If you are serious about your healing journey, stick this piece of paper on your mirror, where you brush your teeth every day. And while you brush your teeth every morning and every night, I want you to take your other hand, place it on your heart, first feeling 3 things you can be grateful for, then and repeat these affirmations, twice a day, every single day.

If you think this is something woowoo, you'd be wrong. There is hard scientific evidence, both from the HeartMath institute, of whom I've studied and interviewed Howard Martin multiple times over the years who is a member of the Transformational Leadership Council who helped Doc Childre found Heartmath, as well as Bruce Lipton, a cell biologist and epigeneticist who I've had the pleasure to interview and learn from multiple times over the years as well.

And the science is clear, placing your hand on your heart, taking a few big deep breaths into your heart, feeling gratitude, and then repeating positive affirmations, activates your healing response, but it also starts to reprogram your subconscious mind to work for you, instead of against.

So please make this commitment to me, and to yourself, right now, that you will do this every day, twice a day, while brushing your teeth. Why brushing your teeth you might ask? Because it's called stacking. Stacking a new habit on top of an existing habit, makes it that much easier for the new habit to stick.

Trying to create new habits in our lives, especially good ones, can be challenging, and there's an entire science to how to create new habits in shorter time, but we're not going into all of those details here - what I will share with you is one of the fastest and easiest ways to create a new habit so it becomes automatic, is to stack it on top of something you already do.

And I created this stacking habit for myself years ago, where I place my hand on my heart, feel grateful, activate the healing response, and then I say my affirmations. The beautiful thing is that it only takes a minute, and we plant two trees with one seed by doing it while we brush our teeth. And since most of us brush our teeth twice a day, we get to benefit from the repetition of this declaration two times, every single day.

So while this might seem like a small and potentially trivial thing, trust me, it's not, it's incredibly powerful and will contribute to your healing journey long term.

So please go do that now. Put the piece of paper on your mirror, commit to doing this twice a day, every single day, while you brush your teeth.

So, to recap, the 3 principles for taking back your own healing power is to recognize and accept that you are your own healer, to be patient with the process, stick to a plan for a minimum of 6 months to a year tracking results, and never give up.

The moment you give up hope or the possibility for healing, is the moment you throw in the towel and tell the cancer that it's won.

And while the healing journey takes time, when you follow through with everything you learn in this book, you will be exponentially more empowered and equipped with proven strategies that assist your body in its own healing.

So, we've finished step one, and now it's time to build your integrative success team. And I'm really excited to help you do this.

Chapter 3

Step 2. Build Your Integrative Success Team: The Synergistic Power of the Right Support Team

As we covered in the introduction, this book is based on 15 years of my own research, experimentation, and interviewing the greatest minds in the fields of health and healing.

In my introduction, we talked about how most medical doctors simply are not taught the foundations of health, and they are unfortunately ill-equipped to help people heal chronic disease.

They are masters when it comes to acute trauma care, like treating a gunshot wound or an organ rupture - but when it comes to metabolic, lifestyle related diseases like cancer, they unfortunately are not taught the foundations and principles of both what cause cancer, and how to eliminate it.

Now there is an exception to this, and those are the medical doctors who recognized in the field of conventional medicine they were practicing, they were not actually helping people heal from chronic diseases like cancer, they were just prescribing more and more drugs, adding more fuel to the fire, and they were awoken to the fact that there is a better way to actually help people prevent and reverse disease, using more natural, holistic and integrative methods, and then they left conventional medicine to actually help people heal, and after decades of first hand clinical experience, they discovered the blueprints for true health and healing, and those are a number of the experts I've had the privilege to spend a lot of time with, and get to share their decades of wisdom and experience with you in this book.

We also talked about the very low bar that is set in the medical industry for what constitutes being a cancer-survivor - and that is, if you are still alive after 5 years from being diagnosed, even if you still have cancer, you are considered a cancer-survivor. The problem with that is that let's say over those 5 years, you are doing conventional treatment, and it completely destroys you, like it did to my Grandpa, who suffered in tremendous pain in the last months of his life, making you debilitated and depressed, and you live past the 5 year mark, you're considered a cancer survivor.

Well we're not going by those incredibly low standards. When I share with you the information and stories from the cancer survivors in this book, they are people who actually became cancer-free, and are living without cancer any longer, using natural, holistic and integrative approaches.

We also talked about the largest study ever done on chemotherapy and how it has a near 98% failure rate, and only a 2.3% success rate, averaged across 22 different kinds of cancer.

And yet chemotherapy, along with radiation and surgery, are the top 3 methods of choice by conventional medical doctors.

And in step 1, we talked about the 3 principles for how to take back your power, activate your innate healing capacity, and be committed to the journey of healing.

I shared with you a very simple yet powerful and scientifically validated strategy that takes one minute every day twice a day to activate your inner healer and take back your power.

I hope you have already followed through with that, and are already practicing it twice a day.

If you haven't read chapter 1 or chapter 2, I highly encourage you to go read them before you move on, they are critical in laying the foundations for your healing journey.

And now, onto step #2!

I'm very blessed to have been building my integrative cancer success team since 2013, and I have dozens of world leading experts, cancer coaches and cancer survivors I can dial at the touch of a button if I have a question or concern about anything related to healing.

Over the years I've interviewed, hosted at my conferences, promoted on my summits, wrote about in my articles, filmed for my documentary; hundreds of experts, from all fields of health, from renowned neuroscientists like Mark Robert Waldman to naturopathic doctors like Dr. Michelle Sands and Dr. Peter Glidden, to holistic and integrative medical doctors like Dr. Leigh Erin Connealy, Dr. Francisco Contreras, Dr. Dana Flavin, Dr. Joel Fuhrman, and Dr. Thomas Lodi, to doctors of oriental medicine like Dr. Robyn Benson and Dr. Nalini Chilkov, to PHDs and MPHs and diabetes experts like Cyrus Khambatta and Robby Barbaro, to emotional healing and behavioral scientists like Marisa Peer, Gregg Braden and Bruce Lipton, to energy medicine and spiritual masters like Donna Eden,

Master Mingtong Gu, Lee Holden and Dr. Roger Jhanke, to cancer survivors like Elaine Gibson, Chris Wark and Dr. Veronique DeSaulniers, and the list goes on and on.

At the touch of a button, literally, I can have just about any major health expert on the planet on the phone, on email, via text or a video conference, and ask them anything I need to know about health and healing.

I am so confident when it comes to healing chronic disease that I know I and my family will always be covered. Whether someone in my family were ever to get diagnosed with cancer, diabetes, heart disease, autoimmunity, or neurodegenerative disease, I know we can get access to the greatest minds in the world, who work hands on helping people reverse chronic disease every single day.

I'm not saying this to boast about my status, I'm saying this to help you recognize that what I'm sharing with you in Step 2 is incredibly important for you if you want to have the confidence, the knowledge, and the support system needed in battling any disease, especially cancer, and it's something I've personally been doing for years, not only to educate myself and my family and help us live as healthy and as long and happy as possible, but to help share centuries worth of hard-earned wisdom with more people around the world, shortening your learning time exponentially.

That doesn't mean you have to go out and spend thousands of hours researching, sifting through and curating information from hundreds of experts and survivors compiling their wisdom and expertise like I have, the good news is I've done a lot of that legwork for you, but what step 2 is all about is making sure you have at least 3 experts in your corner at all times to lean on, glean information from, and support you through the challenging times.

Why 3? Can you have more than 3, or less than 3? The simple answer is, yes! But having at least 3 experts in your corner on your integrative cancer success team is important for a few main reasons, the first is that if someone is not available when you need them, you have backups to call upon. When shit hits the fan, which when dealing with any kind of chronic diagnosis, it certainly can from time to time, having an additional support team to call upon will not only reassure you, but help you stay on track with your healing plan. (And yes, by the end of this program you will have mapped out an entire healing plan specifically for you to follow as you move forward on your healing journey.)

The second reason is that 4 minds working together for your betterment, (your mind, plus 3 others) is always better than 1. When we sit down by ourselves, meditate calmly, and focus on finding the solution to a challenge, we can always get answers. I've done this for the past 15 years, and it's incredibly effective.

But the simple truth is, we're not always able to be calm, centered and focused, especially if something fearful, annoying, painful, or aggravating is bothering or distracting us. That takes years of practice to be able to calm yourself in the middle of chaos, pain or intense emotional challenge. Is it possible, absolutely! I've trained myself to do this over the past 15 years, is it achievable overnight, or in only a few months, maybe, but not likely.

And even so, with this ability to calm myself in the midst of chaos, I still have, and will always have a success team around me to learn from and lean on for the rest of my life. And I really believe you should too.

What happens when multiple minds come together to work towards a common goal? We call that a mastermind, and to join a mastermind group can cost hundreds, even thousands of dollars a month. Whether it's a health mastermind, a business mastermind, a financial mastermind or a political mastermind, it has been one of the surefire ways, for thousands of years, to achieve monumental tasks, in a short period of time - and reversing cancer, can certainly be a monumental task, depending upon how far along you are.

That's one of the reasons I built the Health and Healing Club - so the everyday person dealing with chronic disease can access all of the great wisdom and expertise that I've been so lucky to have access to for years. The Health and Healing Club allows anyone to get access to all of these experts I've been referencing, every day of the week, listen to the interviews I've conducted with them, ask your own questions, and educate yourself without having to do thousands of hours of research. You login, watch an interview, download a transcript, and move on to the next at your own time. And I've made it accessible to anyone and everyone at literally less than the cost of a cup of coffee per day. This is a great starting point for anyone on their healing journey, and a great resource for everyone wanting to learn the deeper truths, strategies and methods for healing cancer and other chronic diseases - and you can sign up by simply going to HealthAndHealingClub.com

I encourage you to pause this for a moment, go setup a free account at HealthAndHealingClub.com, it will only take you about 3 minutes, and then come back and finish this chapter.

Ok, and now the 3rd reason why you want to have an integrative success team is because you get to learn from a variety of experts who have gone deep into their respective profession. The deeper someone goes into a singular area of subject matter, the more knowledge, experience and wisdom one gains.

So what might your success team of 3 look like? Well, you want to look for 4 key traits for your healing team, which include diversity, expertise, specificity and collaboratively.

For diversity, you want your experts to be diverse in their training background, meaning there's not much good to have 3 naturopathic doctors in your corner since they all have a similar foundational training area of expertise in naturopathy, for more bang for your buck, it would be better to have an ND, a holistic MD, and an emotional healing expert, rather than 3 MDs, or 3 NDs for example.

For expertise, you want experts who have years, ideally decades of expertise in their respective fields, not only doing research and compiling data, but have hands-on experience actually helping people reverse disease.

For specificity, you want experts who are very specifically trained on treating your disease - meaning if you don't have diabetes, you might not need to bring on a diabetes expert, but if you do have diabetes along with cancer, you want to make sure at least one of the experts on your team has expertise in helping reverse diabetes.

And finally you want your experts willing to collaborate and play well with others. You want to make sure your 3 experts are willing to talk to one another, share reports and findings and data with one another, and be open to working together, learning from one another, and helping each other grow not only for your own personal betterment, but for theirs as well.

So what are some questions you want to ask when interviewing experts, you are inviting to join your team? Firstly, recognize that yes! This is YOUR TEAM! You are interviewing them, to join your team, not the other way around, and if they don't like that, then they are not right for you.

Remember, you are the client, you are the patient, it is your life, it is your healing journey, not theirs. If they are someone who is being in true service to you, to their patients, to their profession, and to their oath to "do no harm," then they will listen to you, respect you, and honor your wishes.

And, if all they want to do is push you around, scare you, and command you without listening to you or taking your requests or questions to heart, then they are probably not right for you, so move on! There are thousands of specialists in the world, more than enough to find the ones who are right for you.

So, building an integrative success team, will cost some money, and remember, anything worthwhile, especially when it comes to your health and your life, will take some form of investment, whether time, energy or money, and usually it's all 3 - but what if you can only afford one expert on your team? Then make sure they fit all 4 key traits of; diversity, expertise, specificity, and collaboratively. A great example of someone who fits all 4 of these key traits is Dr. Leigh Erin Connealy. She is an Integrative MD with a large integrative healing hospital in California. She not only has the ability to treat patients using the latest medical procedures, but she herself has an entire team of health professionals that you get access to when you hire her, everything from nutrition and exercise experts, to naturopaths, lymphatic massage, ozone therapy, and more.

And that's also true for Dr. Francisco Contreras, who has an integrative hospital in Mexico. And again it's true for Dr. Thomas Lodi who has integrative cancer centers in Arizona, as well as Thailand.

Now, back to money, working with these doctors might not be cheap, as you not only get their expertise, but you get their incredible team and their millions of dollars' worth of advanced healing equipment.

Would it be more affordable to go with one of them and their team, than it would be to get conventional treatment from a regular oncologist who only knows drugs and surgery? In many cases, yes. And even if you don't get treatment from them at their facilities, they, just like many others such as Dr. Peter Glidden, Dr. Nalini Chilkov, Dr. Joel Fuhrman, Dr. Rashid Buttar, Dr. Dana Flavin, Elaine Gibson, and more can coach you over the phone or video conferencing, to help guide you through your healing journey.

And coaching and consulting costs pennies compared to in person treatment.

But if it were me, and I were building a 3-person team, here's the 3 main experts I want on my team:

1. An integrative, functional, or holistic MD. Why? Because an MD has access to certain aspects of medicine that no other expert or doctor can access. And why holistic (H)MD or an integrative MD or a functional MD, because they have extensive training in natural medicine on top of their conventional medical training, so when you are talking with them about diet, exercise, herbs, supplements, energy medicine and so on, they won't look at you like you're a blue alien from another planet.

Some fantastic MDs I know and who are part of the Health and Healing Club and who I personally trust their advice are Dr. Joel Fuhrman, Dr. Rashid Buttar, Dr. Leight Erin Connealy, Dr. Thomas Lodi, Dr. Francisco Contreras, Dr. Antonio Jimenez, Dr. Sunil Pai, and Dr. Dana Flavin.

2. The second expert I want on my team is a naturopathic doctor otherwise known as (ND), or a DOM, otherwise known as a Doctor of Oriental Medicine. Why? Because they are much   more extensively trained in natural medicine, therapeutic botanicals, ancient medicines, and effective plant-medicines that have little to no side effects and can help you heal naturally and live longer without the harmful toxins modern medicine has.

Some great NDs or DOMs I know personally are Dr. Nalini Chilkov, Dr. Michelle Sands, Dr. Roger Jhanke, Dr. Daniel Nuzum, and Dr. Veronique DeSaulniers - all who are part of the Health and Healing Club as well.

3. And the 3rd expert I want on my integrative success team is an emotional healing and /or spiritual healing expert. Why? Because one of the most important aspects of healing cancer, as you'll learn deeply about in step 3, is mental/emotional/spiritual healing. Someone trained in transpersonal psychology, hypnosis, and subconscious reprogramming, is ideal. This is not easy work, and it's not something for the faint of heart, but if you truly want to heal, and find inner happiness and inner peace, ultimately leading to physical healing as a by-product, it is absolutely a necessary part of your journey.

Some great examples of experts who embody these traits are Marisa Peer, Master Mingtong Gu, and Tara Brach.

So when designing your team, put some careful thought into it, make sure they fit these 4 key traits, and then during your interview process of them, ask these 9 interview questions:

1. Have you successfully helped anyone else with my stage of disease, reverse it completely?

2. What were the key areas that you focused on that helped that person reverse the disease?

3. How long did it take?

4. What are your main areas of focus and expertise as a professional?

5. What kind of support and treatments can you help me with even if I can't come to your clinic in person?

6. I am building my integrative success team, and I'm looking for experts who are willing and open to collaborate with other experts - of course following all the HIPAA laws, but to share information, data and reports with one another based on my personal request, and work together to not only help me find my best healing path, but to help all of us learn and grow in the process. In short, are you willing to collaborate with other experts that I bring onto my team?

7. What kind of cost am I looking at long term working with you? What financial options do you have? Do you take insurance? What forms of insurance do you take and what do they cover?

8. Do you have an option where I can call you at any time if I'm having an emergency, or need an expert to talk me through an important decision?

9. If we started working together today, what are the first steps you would have me go through?

Then, after asking all of these questions, make sure you write down the answers in your notebook so you can refer back to them, include the name and contact info of the expert, and then let them know you're interviewing other experts and you'll get back to them with additional questions.

You don't have to make a decision on your first call. And I encourage you not to. I encourage you to make the call, ask the questions, then take some time before you decide. This will give your own inner reasoning and intuition some time to assimilate the information you've received from the phone call.

So where can you find experts that meet all of the standards and key traits we're talking about? You can simply search online, or you can go inside the Health and Healing Club, and start listening to the experts, and choose the ones you resonate with the most. Go to HealthAndHealingClub.com and set up your account right now if you haven't already so you can immediately get access to dozens of world leading experts in all fields of medicine.

And please, don't skip over this part of building your integrative success team. It is so important, and even if you only start with one expert on your team, it is critical that you have someone you can trust, someone you can get checkups and lab results from, someone you can call and ask questions to, someone who can help guide you through the challenging times, if even only once a week, or once a month.

You can even find someone locally who you can go in and speak with and get testing done from time to time, or you can work with experts remotely, using zoom or skype, and send your testing in via snail mail. With the internet it's so easy nowadays to work with anyone just about anywhere in the world.

Dr. Dana Flavin, who is usually in the UK, works collaboratively with doctors all over the US to help patients implement effective integrative treatment protocols, and she is amazing, and one of the most incredibly well informed, well caring, and affordable people you could ever work with. Tell her I sent you if you decide to get in touch with her, she'll take great care of you!

Now, even while building your team, I strongly urge you to continue going through this entire book, all the way to the end, because what you'll learn over the coming chapters will give you the foundations needed when deciding which experts to have on your team, what diet/nutrition/exercise/supplements/ and treatment protocols are used by the best minds in the natural and integrative cancer fields, and what you should be focusing most of your time and energy on during your healing journey.

The remaining chapters in this book are also designed to layout a map for you, a blueprint if you will, one that is informed by my 15+ years in the natural health field and thousands of hours of research and interviews from the world's leading experts on the planet.

This blueprint is not a guarantee cure, but it is a foundation, based in science, that will give you the pillars for creating ultimate health in your body, and give you a fighting chance at turning this diagnosis around, and at the very least, add more years to your life, and add more quality of life to those years.

And what if you simply can't afford hundreds or thousands of dollars a month it might cost to have 3 incredible experts on your team? Well, that's exactly one of the main reasons I've created this book, to make this information accessible and affordable to everyone, no matter the circumstance, and that's why I've also created the Health and Healing Club, so you can get access to the same experts I have access to for less than a cup of coffee a day. So make sure to finish every single chapter of this book and then fill out your Holistic Plan for health and healing in step 7, and you'll have a customized blueprint for your personalized healing journey.

Feeling supported yet? Feeling like you're not a blue alien from another planet? I hope so. I really do. I hope you're beginning to recognize that cancer doesn't have to be scary, that even though we all know we're going to die, there are solutions available to you that can extend your life, and make your life more enjoyable and meaningful in the process.

And that's exactly what we're going to dive into in the next section. How to train your mind and body to get out of fight or flight mode and start creating parasympathetic mastery, the mastery of your parasympathetic nervous system, which is the system that must be turned on as often as possible for your body to heal itself.

So if you're ready, let's dive into the science and practical application of the nervous system to start accelerating your healing journey today.

Step 3. Trade Fight or Flight for Heal and Thrive: Parasympathetic Mastery

W e've already covered a lot in the first 3 chapters. Accepting and overcoming the fear of death as we covered in chapter 1 is critical to your healing journey. The 3 principles and the practical strategy I taught you in chapter 2 is foundational for helping you take back control of your health and support you in moving forward on your path of healing. And the 4 key traits, 3 expert qualities, and 9 interview questions I shared with you for building your integrative success team in chapter 3 are essential in helping you achieve success.

Now, in chapter 4, we're going to dive into one of the most impactful aspects of healing, and that is your nervous system.

Your nervous system can be your best friend, or your worst enemy. The choice is truly yours! And it's either life or death. Getting this one right is that important. But how do we understand the complexities of parasympathetic vs sympathetic?

Innate immunity vs adaptive immunity? Central nervous system vs peripheral? Well, here's the good news; you don't have to know everything about the nervous system or the immune system or the central vs peripheral, parasympathetic vs sympathetic, to understand how it works and what you should be doing to optimize it.

While that is your choice, it's not necessary. Tons of scientific researchers, dating back hundreds of years, have already done most of this legwork for us, the complicated part is sifting through the data and understanding what it all means, then putting a practical plan into place to optimize your nervous system so you can enjoy the healing benefits of being in homeostasis as often as possible, and that's what I'm going to do for you in this section.

I've spent 15 years already sifting through this data, interviewing hundreds of world leading experts and cancer survivors, and spending thousands of hours researching and experimenting. So, my job and my passion is to keep it as simple and straightforward for you as possible. Without getting into too much scientific jargon and data, I want to give it to you simply so you don't get lost in "paralysis by analysis" and information overload - with that said, there are some key elements you do need to understand about the nervous system so you know how it functions and how you can optimize it - so let's lay out the basic framework, and then we'll get into the step by steps that allow your body to be its own best healer. Sound good? Great, let's dive in!

The nervous system is composed of the central nervous system which is made up of the brain and spinal cord, and the peripheral nervous system, which is made up of nerves that branch off from the spinal cord, extending to all parts of the body. Pretty easy, right?

Within your nervous system, you have the parasympathetic and sympathetic responses, these are critical to understand how they work and how they could be working against you - para meaning to go beyond, and sympa coming from the greek root of pathos, meaning feelings or emotions.

Then you have the innate immune system, and the adaptive immune system.

Innate immunity refers to nonspecific defense mechanisms that come into play immediately or within hours of an antigen's appearance in the body. Antigen is just a fancy word for toxin, or a foreign substance that enters the body. These mechanisms include physical barriers such as skin, chemicals in the blood, and immune system cells that attack foreign cells in the body. This includes immune responses like coughing, enzymes in the tears, fever, stomach acid and mucous - all a natural and healthy part of your body doing its job to help remove invaders.

And adaptive immunity refers to antigen-specific immune response. The adaptive immune response is more complex than the innate. The antigen, otherwise known as toxin or foreign substance, first must be processed and recognized. Once an antigen has been recognized, the adaptive immune system creates an army of immune cells specifically designed to attack that antigen. Adaptive immunity also includes a "memory" that makes future responses against a specific antigen more efficient.

For example, if you come into contact with a form of the flu or virus for the first time, your body, depending on how well your immune system is functioning, will get to work producing immune cells to attack and remove that virus. If your immune system is functioning at it's highest capacity, you will likely never even experience symptoms, or if you do, they are very minimal.

If your immune system is not working at its highest level, then you will likely feel very sick, and if your immune system is severely compromised, you can die from that virus. Which is why the majority of people who have died from Covid, are elderly who have multiple chronic diseases and compromised immune systems.

But once your body makes antibodies, and you survive the antigen, then when you come into contact with it again, you are exponentially more likely to kick it out of your system without any symptoms, hence the term asymptomatic.

B cells and T cells are the major **types of lymphocytes involved in adaptive immunity**. B and T cells can create memory cells to defend against future attacks by the same pathogen by mounting a stronger and faster **adaptive immune response** against that pathogen before it can even cause symptoms of infection. Additionally, T cells and B cells are responsible for killing cancer cells.

And finally, you have the lymphatic system. The lymphatic system is the superhighway for removing cancer cells, cell waste, and pathogens from your body by generating white blood cells to seek and destroy pathogens and abnormal cells in the body.

Within these systems you have all your organs that play a role from the liver that cleanses the blood and removes chemicals, to the heart that pumps the blood, communicates with the brain, and produces hormones, to the intestines that host trillions of bacterial and viral cells that host nutrient metabolism, maintain structural integrity of the gut mucosal barrier, modulate the immune system, protect against pathogens, and so much more.

Yes, there are much more detailed aspects to the nervous system, the immune system, the lymphatic system, and so on, but they're really not necessary to go into detail here as we mainly need to focus on the key elements of the systems that both; cause cancer and eliminate cancer, to help you move beyond fight or flight into heal and thrive.

In addition, in steps 4, 5, and 6 we will be going into more detail and specific steps you can take to enhance all your bodily systems that contribute to maintaining a regenerative, wholesome and healthy body.

But for now, let's focus on the sympathetic and parasympathetic responses of the nervous system. Do me a favor and write these down real quick side by side on a T-Chart, like this example.

On the left-hand side at the top, we're going to write Sympathetic.

And on the right-hand side at the top, we're going to write Parasympathetic

Then under each one, here's what we're going to write (start on sympathetic, then move to parasympathetic)

Under sympathetic on the left-hand side, we're going to write Survive.

And underneath that we're going to write Fight or Flight.

Then under that let's write Adrenal response

Then under that, let's write Anger, fear, stress, anxiety, resentment

Then under that, let's write, disease.

Then, on the right-hand side, we're going to write underneath Parasympathetic

Thrive

Then underneath that we're going to write, Rest and Digest.

Then under that we're going to write Immune Activation

Then under that we're going to write, compassion, love, peace, happiness, gratitude

Then under that, we're going to write, Health and Healing

Sympathetic	Para-Sympathetic
Survive	Thrive
Fight or Flight	Rest and Digest
Adrenal Response	Immune Activation
Anger, fear, stress, anxiety, resentment	Compassion, love, peace, happiness, gratitude
Disease	Health and Healing

So, now that we've identified the main differences between Sympathetic, vs Parasympathetic - which aspect of your nervous system do you think you should have turned on and activated the most often?

That's right, your parasympathetic.

And here's the biggest differences. The sympathetic nervous system, otherwise known as fight, flight or freeze, otherwise called by my friend and colleague Bruce Lipton as the adrenal system, is meant as a survival mechanism. If you're in a car crash, and need to bust out of the window before the car explodes, or your child is trapped, and you need to use all your power and strength to save them, or someone is chasing you and you need to run for your life, or a predator is nearby and you need to freeze and remain absolutely still so they don't see you - it's all about survival.

When the sympathetic nervous system is kicked on, your body releases stress hormones such as epinephrine and cortisol, your heart rate increases, you have an increase in cardiac output, blood gets sent to your arms and legs so you can function more effectively if you need to run or fight back, blood flow reduces to the intestines, suppression of insulin happens, and the biggest kicker of all - your immune system and anti-inflammatory response gets deactivated.

Again, listen to this last part - When the sympathetic nervous system is kicked on, your immune system and anti-inflammatory response gets deactivated.

Now, sympathetic fight, flight or freeze is great, for a short period of time, because to save your life from a catastrophic event, your body takes all the energy away from the immune system, and puts it into what's needed like your extremities and your adrenaline in that moment to save your life, or save the life of someone you love.

But how often do you find yourself in a life threatening situation? Not very often, right? But then why is the sympathetic nervous system turned on most of the time for most people today?

We'll cover that in just a moment, but here's the important take away, we were designed to have the sympathetic nervous system activated once in a blue moon. (And yes that's a highly advanced scientific term - blue moon, look it up) And we certainly weren't designed to have it activated every day, which is happening right now to most people who live in the modern world. Why?

People are living in a sympathetic state majority of their waking hours due to 2 main reasons:

Reason #1 - Watching the news. The news is meant to induce low levels of fear and anxiety in the viewers. Why? Because their scientists and marketing experts have told the executives that when people have constant states of low levels of anxiety, shock, and fear, they will not only watch longer, but they will become addicted, and watch every day. Don't believe it? Stop watching all the news right now. Don't watch it, read it, or listen to it on tv, newspapers, or radio ever again.

Could you do it right now without question?

Unless you've already done this, it seems challenging, right? And that's because you're addicted, and they've made it addicting on purpose. I know, nobody likes being told they're addicted to something - but the truth is, if you have hesitation at all, and have fear or anxiety or doubts enter your mind when thinking about stopping something, whether it's sugar, smoking, alcohol, or the news, then it is a form of addiction.

And the news executives love this! They love us being addicted! The more viewers mean the more advertisers; the more advertisers mean the more money the networks make. It's truly all about money, it's not about news any more.

They have made it feel like if you stop watching the news, your life will end. You will not have any connection to the outside world, you'll be left in the void, and you'll have no idea what's going on in the world around you. That thought alone creates fear, and that fear keeps you watching so you'll be stimulated by more fear. It's a vicious cycle, one that we have to learn to get out of if we truly want to heal.

But do they only show negative, scary, violent stories that instigate low levels of fear, anxiety and worry? No, only about 80% of the time! Why? Because they've also found that if they never show something positive, like a cat being saved from a tree, or a funny YouTube video, or a local business owner opening their doors and giving free food to the homeless on Sundays, then without that positive hit of dopamine once in a while, they would scare people straight, meaning they would eventually stop watching the news.

So with the majority of stories being about fear, violence, and negativity, and a small portion being something positive to give you a little lift from all the negativity, they keep viewers addicted for decades.

But why is this important? And does it actually affect your health? The answer is emphatically yes! It's because every time you feel slightly anxious, angry, upset, sad or afraid, your sympathetic system is kicked on, which means your immune system is turned off - and as Dr. Thomas Lodi says in my award winning documentary film titled; Cancer; The Integrative Perspective, he says, "there is a cure for cancer, it's called your immune system."

When you have a fully functioning immune system, your body will remove cancer, exactly as it's designed to do. But when your immune system is not functioning fully, cancer finds its way through the cracks, and proliferates.

So watching, listening to or reading the news every day puts your body into fight or flight, even on a subtle level, and your body doesn't have the opportunity to go into its natural healing state.

Then you leave for work and get upset by the traffic. You have a client call and cancel their account, making you feel worried for your financial future. You see your phone bill and cringe because it's higher than you expected. You open a letter and it's from a debt collector. You fear for your financial security and worry if you will have enough money to live for another 5 or 10 or 15 years.

And so it's not only the news, is the compounding effects of all the negative stories from the news on top of all the little stressful situations you find yourself in every day.

And that's what leads to the sympathetic, fight or flight system being activated majority of the time for most people.

So what's one part of the solution? It's actually really simple. Watch the news once a week. Believe me, you're not missing anything. I once went 10 years without watching a single tv or listening to the news even once in those 10 years, and then when I saw the news again after 10 years, they were literally saying and reporting the same negative types of stories they were 10 years earlier, it's was the same story different day kind of scenario. Like seeing something from the twilight zone.

Now, by only watching the news once a week, you are giving your sympathetic system time to harmonize during the week, and get out of the constant fight or flight mode it's been programmed to be in.

Set a day and time to watch the news, whether it's Sunday at 5pm, or Monday at 7am, but make that the only day and time of the entire week you allow yourself to watch the news. And don't cheat by reading the newspaper or listening to the radio.

When I listen to the radio, I have 5 stations I cycle between. The moment the news or commercials come on, I've trained my nervous system to immediately hit another station, I don't even have to think about it, it's automatic because I've been doing it for so long.

And when I want to see what's going on around the world, or in our country, I check on multiple news stations, once or twice a week, max. The problem is, all news outlets are politically biased. So if you think you're getting the full truth, you're mistaken. They only tell you half-truths.

Don't believe it? Test it yourself. Turn on CNN (left winged news) and watch them report on politics. Then immediately after, turn on

Fox (right winged news) and watch them report on politics. They will take the same exact event, exact same situation, but flip the narrative to support their biggest advertisers and their main audience's political viewpoints.

I'm sorry but that's not news, that's manipulation.

So when I want to know what's really going on, I will watch left wing, then right wing, then slightly more down the middle like PBS, then I'll dig deeper through some internet research and interviews, watching experts from both sides speak. It's sad, but it's the only way we can get the full picture of what's really going on in our world.

If we took the money out of news, stations would start reporting real news again. But we're not there yet, so we each have to be diligent about what we allow in our minds and our bodies via these information gateways.

The second thing to do to overcome the debilitating effects of negative informational influence on your mind and body, is to fill your mind every day with more positive information than negative information. This will give you a more positive and productive outlook on life in general, and will help your body relax, activate the parasympathetic response, (remember para means beyond) so that's going beyond or above the sympathetic response, and very importantly, the first and last things that should go into your mind every day and every night should be positive, uplifting, happy and peaceful.

We'll get into more details later about what an ideal daily routine looks like to keep your body in a parasympathetic healing state as often as possible.

But remember, the more often your body is in a state of peace, tranquility, compassion, love, gratitude, and happiness, the faster your body will heal, plain and simple. And that doesn't mean you shouldn't put yourself through healthy stressors, like intense exercise, actually quite the contrary, intense exercise is one of the ways your body adapts to stressors and releases endorphins that trigger the healing response, but we'll cover that in more depth in step 6.

The 2nd reason why most people live in a sympathetic fight or flight state is because they are programmed to look at life through a negative viewfinder, as either stressful, hard, competitive, challenging, or impossible. They have been taught that life is an "uphill battle." It's "do or die." It's "early bird gets the worm." It's "little dogs stay on the porch." It's "make it or break it." It's "not fair." It's "only rich people make it." It's "I can't get a break." It's "of course that happened to me." It's "Money doesn't grow on trees." It's "I have bad genes." And the list goes on and on.

How many times have you heard these sayings, or versions of them, when you were a kid, or even as an adult? These ideas, when heard enough, or experienced in your physiology through emotion and repetition, become our beliefs, and these beliefs cause us to take actions that continue to support these beliefs. To change our lives, we have to change our beliefs, and to change our beliefs, we have to know which beliefs are sabotaging us.

I've often heard Bruce Lipton explain, "if you want to know which beliefs are sabotaging you, look at your life. Which things come to you easily and gracefully, without much effort? Those are positive beliefs that support those areas of your life. And which areas of your life do you always seem to struggle with? Is it your health, or your finances? Is it relationships, or your job? Whichever areas of your life you struggle with, you can be 100% sure that you have beliefs, even, potentially unconscious to you at the moment, that are causing those areas of your life to suffer."

Another belief that causes tremendous stress for people, continuously activating fight or flight, is time - and that destructive belief is "not having enough of it." I watch loved ones torture themselves daily with this belief. They are always rushing, always stressing, always wanting to be somewhere else, be perfectly on time, be there, not here, not accepting life as it is, feeling like they are missing out, feeling like once they get there, they will be happy, but here, now they are not happy.

And it repeats itself again and again... AND I truly feel for them, watching them constantly stressed out, anxious, unhappy because they believe there's not enough time. Once you can let go of your attachment to time, and learn to appreciate every single moment, whether you're where you want to be right now, or not, then life becomes so much more joyful, and a great bonus is that your immune system is kicked on and your body is healing.

Remember, the goal is to keep the parasympathetic nervous system turned on as often as possible. The more often, and the longer it's activated, the more quickly you will heal.

Now, looking at 3 of the most destructive beliefs that sabotage us every day is the belief that we are not good enough, the belief that we aren't loved, and the belief that we don't deserve it.

A great book to read about beliefs is the Biology of Belief by Bruce Lipton. And some additional empowering resources I encourage everyone to listen to are my interviews in the Health and Healing Club with Bruce, with Gregg Braden, and with Master Mingtong Gu.

And so how do we change our beliefs? Well, we have to reprogram your subconscious mind, which is the part of our mind in which our beliefs live. How do we do that? Simple, 3 ways;

1. Repetition

2. Validation

3. Instillation

Repetition means repeating the same belief, the same thought, the same words, the same action over and over again.

Validation means that you confirm your new beliefs to yourself by recognizing when it shows up in your life.

And Instillation means that you instill the belief into your subconscious, so it sticks and becomes automatic. But it's not enough to just say it, as Tony Robbins teaches, and as the Heart Math Institute has proven, you must wire it into your nervous system. How do you do that? By utilizing the combination of emotional energy and physical application.

Here's an example, let's say you want to instill the new belief that your body CAN heal itself, just like the belief we covered and started instilling into your subconscious in step 1 of this book. Well first, you need to acknowledge and write down the new belief. Next, you need to repeat it every day to yourself. And as part of that repetitive process, you need to use positive emotions and physical application to make it stick.

It's this combination, whether through feeling emotions of gratitude while placing your hand on your heart and repeating the statement to yourself every day, activating every area of your brain that generates new beliefs like we practiced in chapter 2 to help you take back your power for healing, or by shouting and jumping up and down, excited, celebrating yourself and your new belief - but for sure, it is proven again and again, that by writing it down, repeating it every day, and applying positive emotions with physical application, is the fastest way to create new, uplifting, positive and healing beliefs in your brain and your body.

And as Bruce Lipton teaches, it's not your genes that determine your destiny, it's the environment in which your genes live, and if you change the environment, you change your genes. And in this case, the environment we're changing is reducing the stress causing chemicals of adrenaline and cortisol, and replacing it with dopamine, serotonin, and endorphins - which are all healing chemicals.

The question we have to ask ourselves is this, do we want to look at life as something that is happening to me or against me, or do we want to look at life that is something happening for me, to support me. The answer to that question changes everything. One person will live in constant stress, fear and anxiety, while the other will live in constant peace, wonder, happiness and joy.

Even with the most positive outlook on life, you will experience stress, that's part of being human, but its power over you is limited, it doesn't last long, and it disappears quickly, returning to a peaceful, happy or content state.

The choice is yours once you understand the power of beliefs. You literally can choose to change your outlook on life, and life can go from a vicious, terminal, unfair disadvantage, to something that is here to support you, awaken you, uplift you, and help you be fulfilled, healthy and happy. I know because I personally went through this transition in my own life.

I went from an alcoholic, lying thieving homeless drug dealer as a teenager growing up in Bozeman MT, who saw life as vengeful, hateful, and hurtful, to a sober, honest, loving caring father, husband and teacher who sees life as beautiful, supportive, meaningful, and enjoyable.

Do I still experience challenges? Of course. A number of years back I lost my business, got sued by my partner, went half a million dollars into debt, unintentionally hurt my Mom financially, lost my house, moved my wife two kids and two dogs into a small RV, pissed off a lot of people, and seemingly lost everything I had built up until that point.

Did I let that stop me? No! I regrouped. I Meditated. I went inside my mind and heart. I built upon my years of personal strategies for overcoming challenging situations. I discovered my lessons and learning opportunities from the experience. Focused on what I truly wanted. Continued improving my own belief systems around life, money and business, and rebuilt from the ground up, now stronger, wiser, more financially secure and healthier than I've ever been.

I could have laid down in the dirt and let life stomp all over me. But I realized it wasn't life doing it to me, it was my own experience needed to help me gain more mastery over my life, my business and money, which I hadn't learned how to do very well up to that point.

I'm here to tell you that life is truly a beautiful thing when we understand that at its nature, it's harmonious and collaborative, not competitive and evil. Viktor Frankl in his book Mans Search for Meaning, talks about how losing one's humanity in the Aushwitz concentration camp during Nazi Germany, he and other prisoners would find opportunities within themselves to see the beauty and the laughter and the meaning and purpose amidst the terror, even if only for a few moments a day watching a sunset, or looking out over the horizon, or watching some grass sway in the wind - all this while they were beaten, starved, and murdered unjustly - some prisoners were able to see beyond the pain and suffering, to find the beauty and grace of life.

And once they were able to hold onto something to live for in the future, whether it was seeing a loved one again, or having a book to finish writing, or a project to work on once freed, or something that could give them any sense of meaning and purpose, they were able to hold onto life, in even the most devastating, terrorizing, unjust human experience one could ever imagine, and prolong their lives beyond what science thought was even possible at the time, with 0 nutrients, not enough calories to feed a rabbit every day, constant fear and brutality, extreme working conditions and constant exposure to pathogens and sickness.

And there's a lot of similarities we find among cancer conquerors, especially in their mindsets.   Every person I've met or interviewed over the years who has overcome cancer using these methods I'm sharing with you, all have told me, "cancer was a wakeup call, it was a blessing. It helped me realize that I needed to take better care of my health, it made me focus on what truly is important in my life. It made me a better partner, a better parent or grandparent, a better friend."

Dr. V told me that as a Naturopathic doctor, she couldn't believe it when she was diagnosed with breast cancer. How could someone like her get cancer? She was doing "everything right."

But when you've been in this field long enough, and talk to enough people, you come to realize, when someone thinks they're doing everything right, but gets a cancer diagnosis, they're clearly missing something. And for Dr. V, when I asked her what she knew intuitively was the main cause of her cancer, she instantly knew, as many people do, she was working too hard, stressed too often, not taking enough care of her mind, body and emotions.

Even if you have the best diet, you exercise daily, you have air purifiers and alkaline water, you take Epsom salt baths and do infrared saunas - when it comes to the power of the mind and emotions to either cause cancer, or reverse it, there's nothing as powerful.

When the sympathetic fight or flight system is activated due to stress, fear, anxiety, worry, anger, sadness or jealousy, your immune system is turned off, and you create the perfect environment for cancer to grow.

Now, imagine bathing in those stress chemicals for multiple hours every single day, for multiple months every single year, for multiple years every single decade, guess what... cancer is imminent.

Elaine Gibson, 2-time cancer survivor, when I asked her what she did differently the second time to fully heal from stage 4 cancer, that she wasn't doing before, she told me that she began meditating, and meditating for about 2 hours, every day. Again, even though she was doing everything right physically, she was missing one of those most important aspects of healing, and that is keeping the mind, brain and body in a parasympathetic state as often as possible - and that's exactly what meditation does.

Dr. V, one of her most important steps she has identified, and coaches thousands of women in helping them with cancer, that she states helped her tremendously to reverse cancer, and live life with more joy, health and energy, is to heal emotional wounds.

If we want to heal physically, we have to heal emotionally. To heal emotionally, and keep our bodies in a state of parasympathetic response as often as possible, there are 3 effective ways we can do this.

1. Meditate daily

2. Practice energy medicine and ancient healing practices like Wisdom Healing Qigong / yoga / and breathwork

3. Do subconscious healing work through hypnotherapy

Guided meditation, breath work, mindfulness and visualization practices are all scientifically validated forms of calming the fight or flight response, and activating the healing response within your body.

Which ones are the best ones? The ones you will do! Those are the best forms of meditation. If you won't do them, it doesn't matter how good they are. You must consistently practice if you want to see results.

Remember the 3 principles for taking back your power? 1. Become your own healer. 2. Be patient. 3. Never give up. A daily meditation practice is one of the most important tools we have as human beings to become our own healers. And guess what, it's free! Tibetan throat singing, chanting om, yoga nidra, visualization journeys, taoist meditations, qigong meditations, chanting with the Hare Krishnas, Native American dancing ceremonies and sweat lodges, christian mystical prayer, and so on - they are all good! I've spent 15 years experimenting with all of these. Try them. Try different ones. Mix and match. Find something that you enjoy and will stick with.

One of my favorite complete energy and meditation healing systems is Wisdom Healing Qigong, as taught by Master Mingtong Gu. You can find him in the Health and Healing Club, and you can find him online at ChiCenter.com

One of my favorite meditations is sitting at the beach, or in the mountains, watching the sunset. Is that a form of meditation?

Absolutely! It calms the mind, relaxes the nervous system, and activates healing.

I also listen to guided meditations, I practice qigong, I partake in native American ceremonies, I chant with the Hari Krishnas, I practice sound healing, I do all of it. And you can too! And with the internet, you never have to leave your house, if you don't want to. (Even though I prefer to be in person, or out in nature, I also use my phone and listen to guided meditations in the comfort of my own home)

But here's the key, the more progressive your cancer is, the more meditation, qigong, and energy healing you should be doing. Plain and simple. If you expect to drive across the country, on a half empty tank of gas, think again.

When Otis Wallen reversed kidney cancer using Wisdom Healing Qigong and cryotherapy, he was practicing multiple hours every day. When Elaine Gibson reversed stage 4 lymphoma, she not only improved her diet and exercise, but she practiced meditation for one hour every morning and one hour every night.

For how long? For as long as it takes. Remember, be patient, and never give up. Stay focused, stay committed, stay dedicated, and your chances of overcoming cancer will increase exponentially.

And what about deeper emotional healing work like hypnotherapy? This is like taking 5-10 years of meditation and cramming it into (3) 90 minute sessions. Through meditation alone, especially various forms of meditation, qigong, sound healing, and so on, the natural process that happens is that more positive beliefs start to replace negative beliefs, old emotional wounds begin to heal, the body enters a parasympathetic state more often activating the immune system and removing cancer cells from the body, and the mind starts seeing life as beautiful, joyful and supportive. But it takes time. And there's nothing wrong with that.

But if you want to go deep, and go fast, then various forms of hypnotherapy, like Rapid Transformational Therapy that Marisa Peer teaches, is one of the fastest ways. It's also not for the faint of heart. You're going to get into dark and scary emotions you've locked away long ago. You're going to feel them and experience their pain. And then you're going to release them.

But if you choose that path, I strongly urge you to follow through with a minimum of 3 sessions, and make sure to do everything exactly as the therapist instructs you. I've watched some family members do one session, and I noticed a positive change in them immediately, and they did themselves as well, but they didn't follow through with the 30-day process and they didn't do the follow up sessions as they were instructed - and they went back to their old ways.

Emotional healing is like physical healing; it takes time and commitment. Don't sell yourself short. If you're going to do it, then do it fully, no matter how dark and scary. In the end, you will thank yourself for following through because you'll finally be free of the sabotaging beliefs that have kept you stuck in depression and disease for far too long.

And the truth is, you deserve it! You deserve to be happy! You deserve to be healthy! You deserve a great life! How do I know? Because that's my belief! I believe everyone has come to this earth to live a life of joy and meaning and purpose and health and happiness. We all have that God-given right; we just are often missing teachers early in life to show us the way.

But you can have all the health, and joy and energy and vitality that anyone else has. You just have to believe it, and follow through with every step of this program we're going through together, and stay committed to the process.

And finally, before we wrap up step 3, we have to talk about sleep. Why? Because sleep is the easiest, effective, and beneficial way to heal. What happens when you sleep? You guessed it! Your body enters parasympathetic - rest and digest. It enters a state of healing.

But not all sleep is equal. During sleep you have 4 main stages. Awake. Light. REM. And Deep. The most beneficial stage of sleep is Deep. In deep sleep, your body produces HGH, human growth hormone, and releases other chemicals that lead to cellular rejuvenation. The immune system is modulated and your body is in absolute healing mode during deep sleep.

In addition to Deep sleep being the most healing for your body, REM sleep is very important for the health of the brain, and for balancing mood and creating a deeper sense of well-being as well.

Experts recommend that roughly 25% of your sleep is spent in REM and 15-25% is spent in Deep. That means 50% will cycle between light sleep and awake. And awake is actually usually not sitting there consciously awake. These are small amounts of time through the night where your brain and body are awake, even though you are consciously asleep.

But, here's the most important thing about sleep; if your sleep cycle is inconsistent, you don't sleep well or you don't sleep enough, or you do things that cause your sleep to be insufficient, then you're literally shooting yourself in the foot, and missing out on all of the healing benefits sleep has to offer - and remember, sleep is one of the most effective, and FREE forms of healing you can do for your body.

So how do you know how much sleep you're actually getting? You need to use something like Whoop to track it. Whoop, and other heart rate monitors can track your sleep and tell you exactly how much of each stage of sleep you're getting. I promise you will be surprised at the results. I thought I was getting 8 hours of sleep every night because I was in bed for 8 hours, but boy was I wrong! I was only getting 6.5 hours at first! Can you believe that, 8 hours in bed, and only 6.5 hours of sleep!

But over time, as I began optimizing my sleep, the same 8 hours in bed now often equates to 7.5 hours of sleep. I became more efficient, mostly by implementing a couple more of these 7 core sleep principles I already knew, but just wasn't doing.

So if you're committed to getting better, longer and deeper sleep to activate your healing response more often and help you heal faster, I have 7 core sleep principles that you can begin implementing immediately. So make sure to fill in the worksheet in the back of this book so you can reference these each night and make sure you're following through.

Are you ready to go through the 7 core principles? Here we go.

The 7 core sleep principles are:

1. All electronics off 1 hour before bed. This is the minimum amount of time, though 2 hours is ideal. Why? Because the blue light from the screens, and the content coming from the electronics stimulates the brain and prevents melatonin from secreting properly. So, 2 hours if you're really dedicated, but 1 hour is the absolute minimum. If you're going to bed at 10pm, then all electronics off between 8-9pm.

2. Replace all light bulbs in the house with blue light blocking orange lights. This is a game changer. And it's based on the same reason as #1 - the blue light from the bulbs causes your brain to stay awake, reducing the production of melatonin, affecting your quality of sleep. These bulbs can be purchased online. I replaced every bulb in my house with blue light blocking bulbs. They are worth it!

3. Get black out curtains in your room, put all electronics in airplane mode, unplug the wifi router, and make sure you have no lights, no matter how small, whatsoever in your room at night when sleeping. Lights from the moon and stars are actually very healthy for your brain, but lights from the streets, neighbors electronics, including EMFs from wifi, can disrupt your natural circadian rhythm, causing less sleep efficiency. So that means clocks, phones, and all electronics turned completely off, so there are 0 lights and 0 EMF stimulation while sleeping.

4. No caffeine 8 hours before bed. This one is huge. If you want to be asleep at 10pm, then no caffeine after 2pm. Even if you think caffeine doesn't affect your sleep because you fall asleep easily even after a cup of coffee, think again. When you start measuring your quality of sleep, you'll find that caffeine inhibits your body's ability to enter Deep Sleep efficiently, and once you stop having caffeine 8 hours before bed, because that's how long caffeine takes to get out of the system, you'll see your sleep quality drastically improves.

5. Follow a daily routine. For the most beneficial sleep quality, and for the harmonizing of your circadian rhythm, it has been scientifically proven that the best quality of

sleep in adult humans is between the hours of 10pm-2am. This is when the deepest and most regenerative sleep happens. If you are missing any of those hours of sleep starting at 10pm, you're missing out on some of your best deep sleep benefits. Additionally, having a routine, where you go to bed and wake up every morning at the same time, and you do it with the same habits such as, brush teeth, use the bathroom, read a book, meditate, fall asleep. And you wake up at the same time every day, your circadian rhythm is optimized and your sleep is deeply enriched.

6. Do not eat at least 2 hours before bed. Ideally, your body should not be digesting food while you sleep. It should be using that energy on healing and cellular repair. The more time you give your body to digest, before you go to sleep, the more your body can repair damaged cells, including cancer cells, while you sleep. And this is one of the reasons why intermittent fasting, giving your body at least 14 hours of non-eating time each day, so from stopping eating at 8pm, and not eating again until 10am, will give you incredible healing benefits that help reduce inflammation and fight off cancer cells.

7. Get 8 hours or more every night. According to the extensive sleep research I've done, 8 hours is truly the minimum any adult should get each night if they truly want to heal. But if you're really far along in cancer, the more sleep the better. If you can get 9 or 10 hours, even better. If you can take a 1-2-hour nap during the afternoon, even better. The more sleep you get, and the better quality of sleep you get, the faster you will heal - there's 0 debate about that among the scientific community. Many of us were raised being told don't be lazy, get out of bed, don't

sleep all day! And while that might have been the norm growing up, the reality is, you need to do the opposite of that advice if you want to heal.

So, to conclude step 3 of your healing plan, which is trading fight or flight for heal and thrive, here's what a daily practice might look like, that you can literally start right now.

A. Start your day with a 1-hour meditation, any form you choose, whether qigong, sound healing, Taoist, Buddhist, Christian prayer, or likewise.

B. Stop watching the news, and only watch it once per week. Make this commitment to yourself and your health.

C. Commit to 3 hypnotherapy sessions with someone like Marisa Peer's Rapid Transformational Therapy, and follow through with all of their recommendations along the way.

D. Read Bruce Lipton's book, the Biology of Belief, and commit to reprogramming your subconscious mind with new positive beliefs that support your healing.

E. Watch uplifting documentaries, inspirational videos, read positive self-help books, and load your mind and emotions with positive thoughts every single day.

F. Commit to deepening and extending your sleep so you can heal faster.

G. Meditate a second time, for one hour, either every afternoon, or every night before bed.

H. Make sure to finish this book as you will learn additional critical elements that will remove the cancer causing toxins from your life and nourish your cells so your body can heal itself.

Remember, the more of these core healing practices you do, the more often you put your mind and body into a state of parasympathetic response, the more often you trade fight or flight for heal and thrive, the quicker and more effectively you will help your body to heal itself.

And you will truly become the healer within! Just remember to be patient and stay committed to the process.

Then, in the next step, we're going to help you remove and reduce all of the cancer-causing toxins in your life, getting to the root cause of disease, and eliminating it so your body can take healing to the next level!

Chapter 5

Step 4. Detoxify Your Life: Remove and Reduce <u>Everything</u> That Causes Cancer

Over the past 4 chapters we've covered everything from taking back your power, activating your own innate healing response, building your integrative success team, and trading fight or flight for heal and thrive - to the incredible healing stories of people like Dr. Véronique DeSaulniers who healed her breast cancer and Elaine Gibson her reversed stage 4 cancer by making some major lifestyle shifts that we talked about in the previous chapters.

I've shared with you how the conventional medical model has a near 98% failure rate using chemotherapy when averaged across 22 major adult malignancies, how 9 of those major cancers have a 0 percent success rate with chemo, and how it's still prescribed to more than 650,000 every year here in the US, even though for most cancers, it's incredibly in-effective.

We also talked about the extremely low bar that is set from the medical world about the standards that define who is considered a cancer survivor - and how it's time to raise those standards exponentially just like we're doing in this book.

I've also shared with you how a number of highly intelligent medical doctors I've had the opportunity to study and learn from first hand over the years have transitioned their practices away from conventional medicine to holistic medicine because they see better results for their patients.

I shared with you a powerful, scientifically proven simple process you can do twice a day that only takes 2 minutes, that activates your healing response and helps you embody self-heling beliefs to support your healing journey. I also shared with you how to build your integrative success team based on principles and values that can contribute to your success.

We talked in depth about the difference between the parasympathetic and the sympathetic responses from your nervous system, and some powerful strategies for how to consciously activate your parasympathetic response as often as possible so your body has the best chance at healing itself.

We've covered all of these topics and more, and if for some reason you haven't read the previous chapters, make sure to go back and read them. They are foundational for helping you live a cancer-free life.

Now, onto chapter 5! This is a life-changing topic that's essential to anyone who wants to reduce their cancer risk. In this chapter we're going to cover how to detoxify your life by removing and reducing everything that causes cancer.

The unfortunate truth is, once you add up all of the products, chemicals, and lifestyle options humans have created on the planet over the past few hundred years, there are an infinite amount of things that can cause cancer.

But the good news is, most of them can be avoided, and at the very least, they can be drastically minimized so your body can do what it was meant to do - heal and thrive!

During one of my interviews with Dr. Sunil Pai, a world renowned integrative medical doctor and founder of Sanjevani, a holistic healing clinic in Albuquerque, NM - I asked him to simplify the core causes of cancer into a short list that gives us major categories for all causes of cancer, and he beautifully put them into 6 main categories, or what I call the 6 core causes of cancer.

They are:

1. Inflammation
2. Elevated Blood Glucose
3. Environmental Toxins
4. Stress
5. Unhealthy Diet
6. Lifestyle behaviors

We covered stress in depth in the previous chapter, but as a recap, continuous stress, anxiety, fear, worry, anger, sadness and depression all lead to cancer by activating the sympathetic nervous system, response keeping your body in fight or flight. How do we solve that? Simple! You must begin doing the things we spoke about in the previous chapter, backed by science, that activates your healing response and upregulates your immune system, which includes daily meditation practices, qigong, energy healing, mindfulness and gratitude practices to turn on your immune system and activate your healing response.

But what about the other 5 core causes of cancer? I have gone into depth, writing nearly 30 pages with dozens of scientific resources about these causes in my book about cancer, but we'll cover them briefly here in a much more condensed format so you can easily know what to watch out for, reduce, and remove from your life as much as possible.

Every single one of these things we will cover has been scientifically proven to cause cancer. They are carcinogenic, meaning cancer-causing, and there's no debating that, it's well understood by the scientific community, what's not well understood by most people, including medical doctors, is the underlying principles and elements that lead to these causes - but one thing is for certain, if you reduce or remove them from your life, your risk for cancer will go down, plain and simple.

So Inflammation - yes, inflammation causes cancer. But not just any inflammation. Not the good kind of inflammation that happens when you sprain your ankle for example. That swelling is your body's natural healing response sending blood and various healing cells to your ankle to help it heal. That's why the old saying of put ice on it, in most cases, is actually wrong. Swelling, or inflammation, for an acute injury, in most cases, is good, so let your body heal. Does swelling from an ankle injury lead to cancer, almost always, the answer is no.

The kind of inflammation that causes cancer is chronic inflammation. From the United States National Library of Medicine (NLM), a published article in the National Center for Biotechnology Information (NCBI) states; *"Recent data have expanded the concept that inflammation is a critical component of tumor progression. Many cancers arise from sites of infection, chronic irritation and inflammation. It is now becoming clear that the tumor microenvironment, which is largely orchestrated by inflammatory cells, is an indispensable participant in the neoplastic process, fostering proliferation, survival and migration.*

Basically, chronic inflammation almost always happens because somewhere inside your body, you have an infection, or damaged tissue, or constant exposure to carcinogenic toxins that keeps the site chronically inflamed. When an area in the body is continuously bombarded by toxic elements like carcinogens, or by infections that don't heal, a destructive process begins to occur. Repeated tissue damage and regeneration in the presence of highly reactive nitrogen and oxygen species released from inflammatory cells, interacts with DNA, causing the cells to mutate and become cancerous.

Your body sends healing cells such as leukocytes to help heal it, but the inflammation persists because you have not addressed the root cause of that infected or damaged area, and you unknowingly keep damaging it with lifestyle behaviors.

For example, it's well studied and scientifically proven that meat and dairy from animal products, especially processed meat, and dairy, causes cancer. There's lots of science for anyone who doubts this that proves meat and all dairy can lead to cancer. And for someone who eats meat and cheese, and drinks milk, they are constantly causing inflammation in the body.

Just like we know smoking will cause lung cancer, and drinking will cause liver cancer, it might not cause it immediately, but enough of it for long enough, eventually cancer will show up. It's just about guaranteed. And even if you know of someone like your great aunt Betsy who smoked and drank and ate fried chicken her entire life, and never got cancer, I would put $1000 on it that if she would have had some extensive testing done, cancer would have been found. She might not have thought she had cancer, because remember, cancer has very few symptoms until the very late stages, and in many cases it can take decades before it's even discovered, but even if she did somehow miraculously regenerate fast enough to avoid cancer, she's in the .001% of people in the world who do that.

Which is why with the onslaught of fast food restaurants, excessive animal product consumption, preservatives, chemicals, dyes, factories pumping out toxic fumes, carpets filled with toxic flame retardants, food filled with pesticides and herbicides, and so on have deeply contributed to the explosion of chronic lifestyle related and preventable diseases like diabetes, heart disease, autoimmunity, Alzheimer's, and cancer!

In the US alone, nearly 2 million new people will be diagnosed this year, and the numbers keep going up.

So with chronic inflammation, your body tries to repair the damaged area, whether it's the intestines, or the liver, or the lungs, and what happens is, it gets inflamed and repaired, inflamed and repaired, inflamed and repaired, and this process, over and over again in the same area, generates cellular abnormalities, breakdowns in the DNA, causing cells to become cancerous.

Remember, if you have a fully functioning immune system as we talked about in depth in the previous chapters, your body is well equipped to remove the cancer cells, it's part of our design, but if your immune system is compromised, and you are in a constant state of inflammation, not only from eating meat and cheese and drinking milk, but you are breathing in VOCs from your carpet, digesting chemicals from your plastic cups, inhaling pollution from the cars, eating chemical-laden foods, stressed out and worried, and exposed to massive amounts of EMFs at home and at work, now your body is bathing in a cancer-soup 24/7, and cancer is inevitable.

Chronic inflammation is the precursor to just about every major disease on the planet, and once you learn how to reduce and eliminate chronic inflammation, you have the foundation for living a cancer-free life.

So let's go through a list of the 12 major players in our modern lives that cause cancer, so you can start reducing and removing as much of these as possible from your life. Go ahead and fill in the worksheet in the back of this book I've put together for you called Cancer Causing Culprits so you can go through your house and your body right after this chapter, and start reducing, removing and replacing these items as fast as you can. They will give you that massive advantage your body needs to accelerate its own healing.

Remember, the more often you are exposed to carcinogens, the more damage you are doing to your body and helping cancer grow. So we've got to get these out of your life as much as possible, and as quickly as possible. You ready, here they are, we're going to go through these quickly together.

1. Plastics. All plastic cups, bowls, and water bottles - anything plastic that you put liquid into, since the liquid is proven to leach out the chemicals from the plastics, and yes even BPA-free plastics leach all kinds of chemicals into liquids. These plastics must go. It's easy, replace them with glass, and this step is done, you've now just eliminated one of the biggest cancer causing culprits in your home, and it is fast, easy and affordable. Again, any plastic cup or container that you put any leftover food or liquid in, the best to replace it with is glass. Now for cookware, get rid of your typical nonstick frying pans since they also leach carcinogens into your food, and replace them with ceramic, or stainless steel.

2. Bedding. All non-natural, non-organic, polyester or other processed material bedding including pillows, sheets, and blankets, must go. Some of the most common chemicals found in bedding today, (and no, they don't have to list these on their tags so you wouldn't know about it unless you dig deep) are formaldehyde, chlorine, pesticides, color fasteners and dyes. Replace your bedding for a simple, 100% organic, chemical-free set of bedding and all of those important healing hours of sleep will be spent free from breathing in the toxic chemicals that conventional bedding soaks into your skin and your lungs.

3. Body care products. Most body care products, especially the green-washed ones, the ones with a coconut and an avocado on the front of the bottle, the soaps, conditioners, shampoos, toothpaste, lotions, deodorants, moisturizers and so on, have dozens of chemicals, many known to cause cancer. But our wonderful FDA, in all their great wisdom, allows them, because they are in small quantities, so they say they are safe, even though we know most of those chemicals cause cancer - the problem is, it's not small quantities when you add it up over the course of a year, or 10 years. The average woman in America absorbs nearly 5lbs of makeup and lotions into her body every year. That's 5 pounds of chemicals, going straight into the bloodstream, directly contributing to chronic inflammation and cancer cell growth. What's the solution? Do what I and my wife and kids did years ago; swap out all body care products for 100% organic, plant-based, non-chemical products. You have to read the ingredients, make sure they are all natural, no chemicals and preservatives, and nowadays because the

demand has increased due to health intelligence, the prices have gone down, making them much more affordable.

Don't wait another minute, go to your cupboards and throw away all the chemicals right now, and go to your local health food store or jump online, and get what you need that only has 100% organic chemical-free ingredients. This is a big one, and it will make a huge difference for your healing in the long run.

4. Animal products. We've already talked about this briefly, but now's the time to get serious. Remove all meat and dairy from your diet. Go ahead, just throw it out now. Your body will thank you in the long run. The next chapter is all about the most healing and rejuvenating diet for preventing and reversing cancer and living longer and disease-free, so not to worry, you'll learn how it's possible to eat incredibly healthy that is also delicious and makes you totally satisfied, just as I've been doing since 2010, but for right now just know, if you want to stop making cancer, then you've got to stop eating meat and stop drinking dairy.

    Still not convinced? Go join the Health and Healing Club today, and go listen to Dr. Joel Fuhrman, Dr. Thomas Lodi, Dr. Jameth Sheridan, Cyrus Khambatta, Ocean Robbins, Chris Wark and Elaine Gibson talk about the detailed science and proof of why we must stop eating meat and dairy. What will you replace meat and dairy with? Simple. Fresh whole plant foods, thousands of possible varieties, from every major healthy food group including legumes, berries, fruits, vegetables, healthy grains, herbs and more. Again, we'll go into depth on the best anti-cancer fighting diet based in science in the next section, and I'm sorry to burst your bubble ahead of time, it is not keto. Ok?! But let's move on!

5. Stop buying processed food. Check all of your dried and packaged foods like cookies, crackers, chips, pasta, ice cream and pizzas, and if the ingredients have names of preservatives or chemicals that sound like they were made in a laboratory, that's because they were. Most chemicals cause cancer. Most preservatives, dyes, sweeteners, and pesticides that you find in processed food either directly cause cancer, or contribute to cancer cell growth.

    The only way to get these out of our body, and allow our bodies to fully heal, is to stop buying processed food, and any packaged and dried foods need to be 100% plant-based, 100% organic, and 100% preservative free. What options does that give you? Thousands! Not to worry, the market for truly healthy food is growing every day because of people like you and I who vote with our dollar. When we buy and grow the foods that are truly healthy for us, companies have no choice but to listen, and not only make more options available, but make them cheaper as well.

6. Reduce sugar exponentially. Sugar feeds cancer cell growth. There is no debate about this. Doctors use radioactive sugar to find cancer in your body. Why? Because cancer thrives on sugar. But our bodies also need sugar to survive, and the biggest difference here is that processed sugar like corn syrup, agave, white sugar, coconut sugar, cane sugar, barley malt, brown rice syrup, caramel, and so on, all spike insulin levels, leading to an inflammatory response, and ultimately feeding cancer cells.

But healthy sugars, sugars that come in the form of carbohydrates in fruit and vegetables and beans and healthy grains like quinoa, are the exact form of sugar our body needs to thrive, and they come with a whole host of minerals, vitamins, and fiber that's needed for our immune system to function at its higher levels.

The sugar you have to reduce is any sugar that is extracted from its original source, and added to a product. When you eat anything packaged, make sure the sugar content is below 5 grams per serving, and if you really want to heal quicker, don't eat packaged foods with added sugar whatsoever. Only eat whole plant foods that have their natural healthy sugars intact.

7. Stop drinking processed drinks and alcohol. Sodas, pops, most sports drinks, even fruit juice are all filled with not only sugar, but also chemicals and preservatives that can lead to cancer. Alcohol is also a known carcinogen, that can absolutely lead to cancer. Remove them completely, and replace them with herbal teas, fresh vegetable juice, and water, water, water! The body needs lots of water to help it heal itself, and fresh fruits and vegetables are not only full of healing nutrients that fight cancer as you'll discover, but they are filled with water that helps your body function at its higher levels of rejuvenation.

8. Reduce EMF exposure. EMFs from WIFI, cell phones and computers have all been linked to an inflammatory response in the body, ultimately contributing to cancer cell growth. While you might not be willing to do away with these completely, you can do a number of things that I do

that will reduce your exposure exponentially. Remember, everything counts, especially when you stack one thing on top of another.

So, stop carrying your cell phone in your pocket or on your body as often as possible. Use a grounding/earthing mat for your feet (it has to be your bare feet) on the mat when working in front of a computer, put your phone on airplane mode at night, and unplug your wifi at night. For example, I hooked my router up to a power strip so all I have to do is click the button off at night, and turn it back on in the morning. That's at least 8 hours a day you are reducing your exposure! That's 2,920 hours per year with significantly less EMF exposure! That's massive! And it literally takes 3 seconds to turn it off at night and back on in the morning.

9. Reduce pollution exposure. You might live in a city, and are exposed to toxic fumes every day. If you have cancer, highly consider moving to the country like Elaine Gibson did. If you can't, or aren't willing to, then make an effort to get outside into a park, the forest, or a hiking trail as often as possible to breath fresh clean air, and fill your lungs and your cells with healthy air that's hard to find in our overpopulated and toxic cities today. Additionally, a NASA study found that 1 plant per 100 sqft of living space in your house will drastically remove the toxins from the air and help you breath clean fresh healing air every day inside your home or office. And there are great air purifiers available as well which help to clean up the toxins from the air you breath every day.

10. Remove pollutants from your water. City water is often filled with heavy metals, lead, chlorine, and even pharmaceuticals, poisons and drugs that have been flushed down people's sinks and toilets and washed from the streets into the waterways, all adding to the onslaught of inflammation in the body. Start with a reverse osmosis filtration system, and ideally, get a water system that puts the minerals back into the water, and you can also get devices that put hydrogen into the water, and devices that make the water alkaline, which are known to help increase antioxidants and reduce inflammation.

11. This is a big one, and might take a little more time and money, but it's important. Carpets. All chemical-based, fire-retardant, carpets and rugs should eventually be replaced with natural woods, not chemical woods, or replaced with organic non-chemical carpets. The VOCs and chemicals that come off the carpets fill the air you breath in the house every day. Yes, a whole bunch of healthy plants around the house will absolutely help, as well as a powerful air filter, but at the end of the day, removing the chemical-filled carpets completely will give you peace of mind, as well as clean air to breath.

12. And here's the final culprit in this list, even though it's not the final toxin that you'll run into in your life, this is huge and one of the most important of all, and that is Mercury. Mercury fillings in your teeth are a known carcinogen, and are extremely dangerous to your body. Mercury causes cancer, and the mercury from your dental fillings excrete into your bloodstream, and add insult and injury to your cells year after year. There's only one way I know of to get them removed, and that's through a holistic dentist or a

biological dentist. Removing mercury fillings can cause toxic excretion, so you need to have someone who really knows what they're doing. But there are lots of stories I've read, documentaries I've seen, and recently interviewed Warren Phillips who is a toxic cleanup scientist on this subject, and it's clear, that once patients get their mercury fillings removed, whole hosts of chronic illnesses can heal, including cancer. So look up a holistic or biological dentist in your area and see about getting that mercury out of your mouth as soon as possible.

So that's it. Majority of the major cancer-causing culprits that make the biggest difference in your health can all be summed up in just 12 major items, and 80% of them are all simple, fast, and free or cheap to do!

So please go ahead and fill in the worksheet in the back of this book, and take the next couple of days checking off as many of these as possible. Once you've done 80% of them you're well on your way to living a healthy and cancer-free life.

Remember, these things are the foundations for true health. If you don't do these simple but powerful steps, how can you ever expect to heal? I know it can seem overwhelming, and I'm asking you to make some serious changes in your life, changes that you may have thought about for years, or changes that you've never thought about, or even knew you should make, until now.

And I know it's not always easy, but trust me, it will be worth it! Removing these cancer-causing elements from your life will not only give you peace of mind, but will give you your life back. And I know that's what you want. You want to feel better, live longer, have less pain, enjoy life more fully....and you can do all of that when you're healthy, right?

Just the fact that you've made it this far in the book tells me you're serious about transformation, you're serious about your health, and you're serious about making the changes necessary to truly heal. So I commend you, and congratulate you, and encourage you to fill in the worksheet in the back of this book, get rid of as many cancer-causing agents as you can right now, then let's move onto step 5, where you'll learn exactly what it takes to nourish and rejuvenate your body, turning your body into a true cancer-eliminating miracle!

This next chapter is critical to your healing journey. As you've discovered, removing the things from your life that cause cancer are foundational to your health, but just as important are putting the things into your body that create true healing and rejuvenation - and that's what we're going to cover next.

Chapter 6

Step 5. Nourish and Rejuvenate: The Most Scientifically Validated Anti-Cancer Solutions

Are you ready for this?! This is one of the most exciting and empowering chapters you'll learn in this book! So now that you've removed many of the toxins from your environment that have been directly supporting cancer proliferation, have begun or enhanced your mindfulness, meditation or energy healing practice, have removed the toxic burden that mainstream media proliferates in your nervous system, and you've began building your integrative success team, it's time to move to step 5, and begin nourishing and replenishing your cells so they not only limit cancer cell proliferation, but help enhance your immune system so your body can get rid of cancer cells much more efficiently and effectively.

Here's a key statement, what you put in or on your body, becomes your body. It's incredibly important to know this for your life. Again, what you put in or on your body, becomes your body.

What goes on your skin - goes in your bloodstream and becomes the environment that your cells live in, and what goes in your mouth - goes into your bloodstream, and becomes the environment that your cells live in. If you put chemical lotions on your skin, drink alcohol or smoke cigarettes, eat meat and dairy, or put conventionally grown produce filled with pesticides, herbicides and fungicides, into your body, that's what your cells are being fed when they replicate, and those chemicals and toxins, become you.

That's why we have to be diligent, every single day, keeping these toxins and chemicals off our bodies and out of our bodies. Got it!? Good! Now this next part is fascinating, and actually very important.

The cells in your intestine replace themselves every 2-4 days. Your stomach; every 2-9 days. Your skin cells, every 10-30 days, your stem cells, every couple of months. Your red blood cells, every 4 months, your fat cells about every 8 years and so on until just about every part of your body is completely new and different than it was months or years prior.

Depending on the area of your body, the cells are going to die off and be replaced by new cells quite often. In some areas this happens much quicker than other areas. Why is this important? Because what you put in and on your body, is what creates the environment in which your cells live, and as world renowned cell biologist Bruce Lipton clearly discovered, it's not your genes that determine the destiny of your cells, it's the environment.

So the most important question is, what kind of environment is both inhospitable to cancer, and is supportive to ultimate health and vitality?

Remember early on in previous chapters when I said I Want to make this as simple as possible for you, because the more complex something is, the less likely we are able or willing to do it, right?

So please note, there's a lot more to these biological processes than I'm going to cover here, but what I'm going to cover are the essentials, so you have a core understanding of the environments in which cancer thrives, and that way we can change the environment in which your cells live and create a healing environment inside yourself that is conducive to healing, longevity and vitality.

So let's grab a piece of paper, and make a T-Chart. On the left, we're going to write cancer, on the right we're going to write, health. Starting on the left, let's write down the 3 foundations of our internal environments which leads to cancer, and on the right we're going to write down the 3 proven principles of health.

Ok, so on your piece of paper, on the left hand side, write down Cancer.

Beneath that, write the word, acidic.

Below acidic, write anaerobic.

Below anaerobic, write the word Stagnation.

Ok, then below those, let's write, these lead to:

Cell fermentation, DNA damage, aerobic glycolysis/ increased glucose uptake.

Ok, now, on the right side of the paper, we're going to write down Health, at the top.

Under that, we're going to write Alkaline.

Under alkaline, we're going to write Aerobic.

Under aerobic, we're going to write Invigoration.

Ok, got those 3?

Now under those three, we're going to write, These lead to:

Healthy cellular respiration and ATP production, Normal DNA replication, and nutrient assimilation. Here's what it should look like.

Cancer	Health
Acidic	Alkaline
Anaerobic	Aerobic
Stagnation	Invigoration
- These lead to -	*- These lead to -*
Cell Fermentation	Stagnation
DNA Damage	Normal DNA Replication
Aerobic Glycoses / Increased Glucose Uptake	Nutrient Assimilation

So let's unpack this and make it as easy as possible to understand and then make applicable in your life, ok?! Starting with acidity and alkalinity. Cancer cells not only thrive in an acidic environment, but they convert the environment around them to become more acidic while they make the interior of their cells more alkaline, so they can survive.

So what is the pH scale that measures how acidic or alkaline something is?

Well your body works constantly to carefully control pH levels of blood and other fluids. The right pH levels are needed for good health, and a pH imbalance will literally mean the difference between disease and health.

The pH scale ranges from 0 to 14. The readings are based around a pH of 7, which is neutral, like pure water for example.

A pH below 7 is acidic.

A pH higher than 7 is alkaline.

This scale might seem small, but each level is 10 times bigger than the next. For example, a pH of 9 is 10 times more alkaline than a pH of 8. A pH of 2 is 10 times more acidic than a pH of 3, and 100 times more acidic than a reading of 4, because it's multiplied by 10 - make sense? So from one number to the next, it's a massive difference in pH.

So, what's a normal blood pH you might ask?

Your blood has a normal pH range of 7.35 to 7.45. This means that blood is naturally slightly alkaline.

In comparison, your stomach acid has a pH of around 1.5 to 3.5. This makes it acidic. A low pH is good for digesting food and destroying any pathogens that get into the stomach.

So, to make it simple, the healthy alkaline pH levels of the external environment of a healthy cell are 7.4 - alkaline. The environment in which cancer cells thrive is an acidic environment, around 6.8. That means that the environment in which cancer cells need to thrive is roughly 6x more acidic than that of a healthy alkaline environment.

Make sense? The basic understanding is this; you want your body to be in an alkaline state as often as possible to help reduce and prevent cancer cell growth.

But here's what's interesting, it's very difficult and rare to actually change your blood pH. Now you can change your urine or saliva pH easily, and that's because your body is constantly optimizing itself through various functions to maintain a normal blood pH, which can cause your urine or saliva to become more acidic - so these are not totally accurate ways to test your pH, though they can give you some insight.

Our lungs and kidneys are largely responsible for controlling the pH of our blood, and it is imperative that it remains between 7.3 and 7.4 for our survival. Based on the types of foods we eat, our body (and the kidneys in particular) needs to do more or less compensating for optimizing our pH levels. However, the actual pH in food doesn't determine a net effect on the body, that's why the Alkaline diet isn't necessarily the cure-all if you will. Rather, the effect food has on the kidneys, called the "potential renal acid load" or PRAL determines where that food fits in the context of the acid-alkaline diet. For example, citrus fruits are acidic but are considered high alkaline foods because they have a low renal acid load.

So here's the important takeaway, we're not necessarily trying to change the pH of your blood, your body does all kinds of functions to create a normal pH in the blood, and if your blood starts showing acidity, major health complications and death would be a near immediate result.

What we want to do is enhance the alkalinity of your cellular environment so that your body has to do less work in balancing its pH, ultimately leading to higher levels of health and healing. Does that make sense? Since cancer cells thrive in an acidic environment, we want to help make the environment of the cells as balanced and naturally alkaline as possible - and, we want to take the toxic load off

94

the body as much as possible so it has less work to do, and less cellular toxicity, so it can focus on cellular regeneration following a normal cellular replicative process.

I'm sure you're already asking the next question, "so how do we make our bodies be in a more balanced alkaline environment?!" Good question! It's actually quite easy. The first 2 steps we've already done, and that is to reduce the toxins in our lives that cause acidity, like meat and dairy, alcohol, smoking, processed food, high fat foods, fried food, processed sugar, artificial sweeteners and fast foods, and yes, you guessed it, even stress can cause acidity in the body.

The 2nd step is to nourish our bodies with alkaline promoting foods. So which foods are known to create alkalinity in the body, making the body inhospitable to cancer? It's what your parents might have told you again and again: eat your vegetables! But it's actually so much more than that!

And please note, again, I'm promoting an alkaline-specific diet here, even though there's a lot of benefits to the alkaline diet, but the reason being is that there are foods that on paper look acidic, like lemons or limes or oranges, but actually have anti-cancer and anti-inflammatory effects, and also have a low renal load which helps to balance alkalinity in the body - and, the reason I'm not promoting alkaline-specific diet is because if we get stuck on alkalinity, and miss all of the beneficial nutritional qualities of a diverse host of foods, filled with vitamins, minerals and phytonutrients, many of which have been well studied and are known to help heal inflammation and fight cancer, then we're missing the boat. Make sense?

So, what is the best anti-cancer diet? Well, in 15 years of research, having spent thousands of hours interviewing hundreds of world leading experts in health and healing, and having spent thousands of hours of researching and experimenting with health on myself, what I have found to be the most proven cancer-fighting foods on the planet, confirmed by decades of hard scientific studies, as most easily explained by world renowned medical doctor and my friend and colleague Dr. Joel Furhman, can be summed up into what he calls G-Bombs. G-Bombs stands for greens, beans, onions, mushrooms, berries and seeds.

There's 3 main reasons why the G-Bombs diet is the best diet for cancer, which is a diet high in thousands of available and medicinal varieties of greens, beans, onions, mushrooms, berries and seeds - and the main reasons are because it is high in fiber, which is necessary for feeding your microflora in your gut responsible for nearly 70% of your immune system, helping produce T-Killer cells that remove cancer. It's high in nutrients that are known to kill cancer cells, have antiviral, antimicrobial, anti-inflammatory and ant parasitic effects - all important elements of making cancer inhospitable. And #3, it's high in alkalinity, helping keep your body's cellular environment at a balanced pH.

In addition to G-Bombs, the research shows we can be adding in a healthy dose of herbs, nuts, and fruit to our diet. While G-Bombs does have berries in it, and some fruits like citrus, and they are some of the most well studied and recognized anti-cancer fruits we know of so far, there are still massive benefits to people with cancer from fruits like kiwi, oranges, avocados, tomatoes, apples and bananas - including high levels of fiber, micronutrients, and alkalinity.

Additionally, there are hundreds of well-studied herbs, like basil, caraway, cinnamon, clove, coriander, cumin, dill, garlic, ginger, rosemary, saffron, and thyme, among many others, that have many anticancer properties. These herbs, if sprinkled on food, is of course helpful, but not therapeutic, especially when trying to reverse cancer.

Therapeutic doses of herbs should be taken for maximum benefit, but I would suggest when taking any therapeutic plant doses that you do it under the guidance of a trained DOM, Doctor of Oriental Medicine, or master herbalist who can guide you and help keep an eye on any potential side effects.

In addition to the seeds that Dr. Fuhrman is speaking of, like sunflower seeds, flax seed, chia seeds, and so on, which are incredibly beneficial to the reduction of inflammation in the body and helping stop cancer cell proliferation, there are a vast array of health promoting nuts like walnuts, pecans, almonds and pine nuts that are known to have anti-cancer effects as well.

When you add it all up you have a vast array of delicious and nutritious greens, beans, onions, mushrooms, seeds, fruit, nuts, and herbs to eat each day.

Do you know how many options for meals and variety that allows you in your diet? Infinite! Literally, infinite options. To date, according to the World Economic Forum, there are at least 200,000 edible plant species on the planet so far. Unfortunately, only about 20 of them make up most people's diets today. If you believe in God, why would God make at least 200,000 species of plants filled with medicinal qualities available to humanity in every corner of the planet, unless we were meant to eat them?! Right?!

Now, one of the best ways you can get the anti-cancer nutrients quickly into your bloodstream, is by juicing. And I'm not talking about what some of the crazy powerlifters do by juicing steroids, ok?! But juicing fresh vegetables is key to your health! Yes, you need the fiber, especially when eating fruit, but when you have cancer, you want as much alkalinity and as much nutrients in your system as possible, as quickly as possible, and as often as possible.

The best way to do that is through fresh green vegetable juice. The most proven anti-cancer vegetables include cruciferous vegetables like Arugula, Bok choy, Broccoli, Brussel sprouts, Cabbage, Cauliflower, Collard greens, Daikon, Horseradish, Kale, Kohlrabi, Mustard, Radish Rutabaga, Turnips and Watercress.

All of these can be juiced, added to salads, soups and all kinds of delicious and healthy plant-based meals.

If I were to break it down, the ideal anti-cancer diet should include at least one large salad every day with a minimum of 5 of these varieties of greens in the salad, on top of adding some nuts and seeds, some dried berries, mushrooms and onions - followed by a low fat, organic vegan dressing made of lemon juice or apple cider vinegar, a tiny bit of olive oil and some sea salt - or any other simple and delicious dressing, low in fat, low in sugar, all organic and vegan.

Then on top of your salads each day, you should eat a large bowl of vegetable and bean soup, with multiple varieties of vegetables, beans, onions, mushrooms and garlic. The legume family, including black beans, pinto beans, lima beans, lentils, soy beans (yes, organic soybeans are incredibly healthy for you and scientifically proven to reduce cancer cell proliferation, and not having harmful estrogens we were once lied to about, despite the misinformation campaign that happened for a couple of decades - the estrogens in soy are phyto, not xeno, and phytoestrogens are actually incredibly healthy) and other kinds of beans are filled with minerals and fiber that help build immunity, strengthen the microflora, and destroy cancer cells. Add in vegetables, onions, mushrooms, garlic and some sea salt, and you have a vital and healthy soup that will make cancer run away screaming!

In addition to the salads and soups, which are important for the fiber and vital nutrients, juicing these cruciferous vegetables every single day is ideal. And drinking as much juice as possible each day will truly benefit your healing. Like Elaine Gibson told me, "once I drank green juice for the first time I couldn't stop drinking it. I became juiceaholic." And I can totally relate to Elaine.

Chris Wark, who reversed cancer on a raw food, high green juice diet, told me that he wanted to try and overdose on vegetable juice. He drank it all day, every day. And guess what! He couldn't overdose, in fact, he completely healed from cancer and then began teaching people all around the world exactly how he did it.

While adding 5 or more of those varieties of cruciferous vegetables to your juicer might not produce enough juice by themselves, and might not taste all that great, here's a little secret to add more nutrients, more liquid, and a better taste to your juice - add in a full stalk of celery, 2-3 cucumbers, 4-5 large carrots, an apple and a beet to your juice. Celery and Cucumber are mostly water, but water filled with nutrients, so they add a lot of liquid to your juice.

Be mindful of the amount of carrots, apples and beets you juice, as once you juice them, you remove the fiber, and you increase the sugar load on your body, (though it is healthy sugar) but add them in sparingly, and make 80% or more of your juice from fresh green vegetables, 20% from things like carrots, apples and beats.

At the end of the day, who cares if it doesn't taste like chocolate pie!? Your body is going to love it, and you'll be creating an alkaline environment filled with anti-cancer benefits to help kick cancer out of your system for good.

For more nutritious and delicious recipe ideas pickup a copy of Dr. Fuhrman's book titled the Eat to Live Cookbook. I have it, I've made a number of recipes from it, and they are some of the healthiest and delicious recipes you'll find anywhere!

Remember, this is not a quick fix. It's not about eating a salad, drinking some juice, and all your problems go away so you can get back to eating and living unhealthy again. This is about a total lifestyle change! It's about a whole-human makeover! One that will add years to your life and quality to those years. One that will give you a glow coming from your face you haven't seen in a long time, it's a lifestyle change that takes commitment, dedication, daily action and follow through.

The more you do, the faster you're going to see results. And don't get down on yourself if you don't get it all right, right away. That's why you have your integrative success team that we helped you build in step

2, so you have someone in your corner helping you stay on track, and someone by your side to help support you through the challenging times.

Ok, so now let's talk briefly about the next two foundations that create an environment for cancer to thrive, and their opposites, which make your internal environment inhospitable to cancer.

In addition to an acidic environment, cancer thrives in a low oxygen environment, otherwise known as anaerobic, and in a stagnant environment, or what we'll call stagnation.

As Ludwig Cancer Research scientist Paul Mischel, MD, who is based at the University of California, San Diego School of Medicine says, "Cancer and other fast-growing cells extract energy from glucose using a process that ordinarily kicks in only when oxygen is in short supply," He also explains that "This allows them to thread the needle: they get the energy they need from glucose but also retain the carbon-based building blocks for molecules like lipids, proteins and DNA, which dividing cells need in large quantities."

It's been proven again and again that a low oxygen environment in your cells opens the door for cancer to form. This causes cancer cells to survive by converting glucose into lactate followed by cell fermentation. Which is why cancer cells thrive on sugar. But they have other ways of thriving even if you starve them completely of sugar, so that's not the only solution.

Yes, we have to reduce our sugar intake drastically, only taking in healthy sugars in the forms of whole plant foods, but our bodies need glucose to thrive, so a ketogenic diet, which is a fad diet promoted by too many health experts nowadays, is one of the worst diets, long term for people with cancer or diabetes. In fact, the hard evidence shows that a long term ketogenic (high fat) diet, even healthy fats, will eventually lead to diabetes. And people with diabetes are exponentially more likely to have cancer due to a number of metabolic factors.

It is true, that a high fat diet, when done properly using whole healthy plant fats like avocado, coconut, nuts and seeds, can help starve cancer cells, burn excess fat from the body by burning ketones for energy, and reduce inflammatory markers - but even the best clinical experts who actually work with cancer patients every single day in their offices like holistic medical doctor Thomas Lodi and Dr. Joel Fuhrman, say the plant based keto diet is a short term therapeutic diet, meant for weeks or months at a time, not meant as a long term health approach.

Dr. Joel Fuhrman, who has helped tens of thousands of people reverse chronic disease through his work also says the ketogenic diet, a high fat diet, is not ideal, or recommended for people with cancer, as it can cause long term health damages that are outweighed by the short term benefits.

So a low fat, whole foods, organic, plant-based, low glycemic, high carbohydrate, moderate caloric intake, moderate plant protein diet is the best for cancer patients. That is roughly 20% fat intake, 15% protein intake, and 65% carbohydrate intake, and the majority of carbohydrates are coming from anti-cancer foods like beans, vegetables, healthy grains like quinoa, fruit and berries.

Even the experts at Mastering Diabetes, who have thousands of people completely reverse prediabtes and type 2 diabetes, based on all 4 markers of diabetes tests available, by implementing a low fat, whole foods, plant-based diet. (10% healthy fats, 10-20% protein, and 70-80% high plant based carbohydrate intake.) If you want to know more about their incredible work with diabetes, and the dozens of scientific studies backing their work, get their book titled Mastering Diabetes, and join the Health and Healing Club where you can listen to my extensive and profound interviews with them highlighting the science behind this living-diet.

And back to cancer thriving in an anaerobic environment which is an environment devoid of oxygen, we must oxygenate our cells, making them more aerobic, so they can efficiently produce ATP, the molecules of energy that create most of the life in our bodies. Oxygen rich foods, oxygen rich water, and oxygen rich air all contribute to oxygen richness in our bodies.

Hemoglobin, a red blood cell protein, helps carry oxygen through your blood. If you want to consume foods that increase oxygen uptake, eat nutrients that support red blood cell production. The more red blood cells you have, the more hemoglobin is available to move oxygen through your body. And those are just about all the foods we just covered.

And the most oxygen rich water available on the planet is if you fill your cup straight from a bubbling spring coming out of the earth, or you collect and drink rainwater fresh from the rain. Additionally, alkaline water is known to help increase blood viscosity and assist in getting morte nutrients to your cells. Some other options are to drink water that has ozone or hydrogen added to the water. These devices can now be found just about anywhere and when they used to be thousands of dollars, now they are only in the low hundreds, affordable and accessible by just about anyone.

Another way to get more oxygen into your blood? Exercise! But not just any exercise, we're talking about the most scientifically proven forms of exercise that help oxygenate your blood and remove cancer cells, all of which we'll go into depth during the next chapter.

Which leads us to one of the most important foundations that lead to cancer cell proliferation, and that is stagnation. Stagnation is death for the body. The body is meant to move, it's meant to jump, climb, run, swim, crawl, walk, bend, lift heavy things, and all kinds of movement. Just as the physical body needs to constantly experience invigorating forms of movement on a daily basis, the lungs need to expand and contract at various rates, from intense to subtle, for efficient oxygen to reach the bloodstream, plus movement is the main pump of your lymphatic system, the system which most efficiently removes cancer cells from your body.

If you don't get invigoration right, then you're missing out on the majority of the FREE cancer healing benefits available to you every single day, and in fact, without proper movement, your body is building up waste products that will contribute to chronic disease.

In the next section, we're going to talk about the 4 forms of movement that are scientifically proven to reduce cancer risk, improve energy, and increase life span. These 4 forms of movement should be done 6 days a week, and they are critically important to your health and longevity.

So, before we jump into step 6, take a moment now, and review these 3 key elements that create the foundations for a cancerous environment and the foundations for a healthy, cancer-free environment.

Again, looking at your T-Chart, cancer thrives in an acidic environment, a low oxygen environment, and an environment of stagnation. These 3 environments are the perfect cesspool for cancer cell proliferation - and they cause cell fermentation, DNA damage, aerobic glycolysis through increased glucose uptake. Basically, what that means is that with a very acidic diet with low levels of oxygen and a lifestyle of stagnation, meaning you don't exercise very often or follow the 4 forms of exercise I'm going to share with you, then you're creating the perfect environment for cancer.

And on the right side of our T-Chart, we have health and healing. And to create health and healing in the body, we need to create an alkaline, oxygen rich, invigorated environment and lifestyle. This lifestyle leads to ultimate health and healing, and is inhospitable to cancer due to healthy cellular respiration and ATP production, Normal DNA replication, and nutrient assimilation.

So, your assignment for this chapter is to order Dr. Joel Fuhrman's book right now titled the Eat to Live Cookbook, so you have all of the healthy recipes you need at the touch of your fingers. If you don't have a juicer, hop online and order one now, I've used Breville juicers for years, but I've also used Jack Lalaine juicers, and for preserving more nutrients, but taking more time to juice and to clean, you can get the cold press juicers. Whatever juicer you get, make sure you use it every day.

Follow my guidelines about which vegetables to add to your juice and start with at least 1 qt per day, working your way up to 3 quarts per day if you really want to heal fast. Once you're on track and seeing major progress, you can back off the juice slightly, but at a bare minimum, 1 qt per day of fresh green juice should be your go-to for the rest of your life if you want health, vitality, and cancer-prevention.

Then go make at least one huge salad using the recipe guidelines outlined before, followed by a large vegetable and bean soup. If this becomes your foundation every day, 1 qt of green juice, 1 giant salad and one large bowl of vegetable and bean soup with onions, garlic and mushrooms, your body is going to get so nutrified you'll be feeling and looking younger in weeks, I guarantee it!

And after a few months of this, you'll be on track to adding more years to your life and more life to those years! And after a couple years of this, following all 5 steps we've outlined so far of this healing lifestyle, you'll be a brand new person, feeling and looking better than you've been in a long time, and maybe, just maybe, you'll revers cancer completely as well.

But as I mentioned, none of this matters if your body is stagnant, s make sure you stick with me through step 6, it's vital!

And before we get to step 6, I need to cover a few more key element of nourishment and rejuvenation before we move on from this chapter And these are some therapeutic approaches that will add icing on th cake for your healing journey.

Some of these are free, and most are incredibly affordable. These are things like taking high dose Vitamin C, high dose Vitamin D, taking magnesium, zinc, curcumin, frankincense, black pepper, Echinacea, vitamin b-12, and probiotics.

Even though you'll find most of these nutrients in adequate amounts inside your food and your juice, aside from b-12 since the bacteria which makes b-12 is washed off all the fruits and vegetables, these are all scientifically proven nutrients, when taken in large enough doses, to enhance your immune system and fight off cancer.

While you can get all of these supplements in pill form, I highly recommend getting them in liquid or powder, to prevent indigestion problems that can come from taking too many capsules at a time. How do you know how much of each you need to take, call up your Naturopath or holistic MD, get a blood test, and then have them walk you through the reports and help you identify which nutrients you should be supplementing with and at how much and how often. Research shows that Vitamin C for example, taken 3-4 times per day, up to 500 mg at a time, is very therapeutic and effective at supporting the immune system and the body through multiple functions, including eliminating cancer cell growth.

It's also well studied that when curcumin, frankincense, and black pepper are taken together, there's an incredible anti-inflammatory benefit that synergistically happens when taking these 3 ingredients at the same time, and we know chronic inflammation causes cancer, so reducing inflammation naturally is a key component in healing, and I highly recommend you join the Health and Healing Club and listen to my interviews with Dr. Sunil Pai about this exact subject. If you're not yet a member, go to HealthandHealingClub.com to learn more about it.

And we also know that getting out into nature away from pollution and EMFs, as often as possible, ideally every day for at least an hour or more a day, is not only beneficial to the immune system, but it helps to reduce stress, activate the parasympathetic nervous system, and generate a healing response.

So, salads, green juice, soups, supplements, water, time in nature, meditation, and reduction to toxins lay the foundation for our cancer-free lifestyle so far, now let's dive into the last main foundational element that ties it all together.

Chapter 7

Step 6. Medicinal Movement, Move Daily for Life

I've spent 15 years researching and learning from the best minds in the fields of natural health, integrative oncology, energy healing, holistic health, spirituality, neuroscience, nutritional therapeutics and behavioral change, and I'm incredibly proud of this book and humbled and honored that you're joining me throughout these chapters.

You know, I remember that back in 2005, I was able to change my own life, overcome years of sickness and addiction, and step into my life purpose while diving deep down the path of natural health. Then in 2013, after my Grandpa passed away from cancer, and not only the cancer itself but the conventional treatment of chemotherapy and radiation, I became obsessed with learning everything I possibly could about cancer, what causes cancer, and how we can heal our bodies from cancer most effectively.

I began interviewing hundreds of world leading experts and cancer survivors. I produced summits, conferences, magazines, online video series and an award winning documentary. I never thought I'd be this passionate about something like cancer, but I am! And I know that once you fully understand and implement the information taught in this book, and all the previous chapters we've covered, it can transform your life, and give you a profound sense of wellbeing, science based healing strategies, and professional support on your healing journey.

And that's why I created this book, so no-one will have to be afraid of cancer again, and so more people can understand what cancer actually is, how we get it, and how to stop making it. And whether you are able to become totally cancer free, or you at least add more years to your life and more quality of life to those years, the foundations, practices, and scientifically validated approaches I have shared so far, and will continue to share over the coming chapters, will give you the confidence, support, and principles you need to live a cancer free life.

I know there's a lot of great resources available about preventing and reversing cancer, but honestly up until this point, I hadn't found this level of depth of not only foundational training, but practical application as well as turning the complexities and scientific understandings about cancer into a simple and effective blueprint for taking back control of your health. So that's why I wrote this book, and I hope you've gotten a lot out of it so far.

We've covered so much in the previous chapters, and if you haven't read them for some reason, make sure to go back and read them all, they will give you a truly transformational and effective approach for turning your mind and body into a healing powerhouse!

Now, if you can remember from the previous chapters, what are the unhealthy lifestyle behaviors that can lead to cancer? They include poor diet, excessive stress, continuous toxin exposure, smoking cigarettes, drinking alcohol, eating animal products and chemical-laden food - but I would argue that the most overlooked lifestyle choice that can lead to cancer and other chronic diseases, is sedentarism.

Many people think they are not sedentary, since they feel like they are constantly moving from the bed to the kitchen, from the kitchen to the car, from the car to work, from work to the grocery store, from the grocery store to school, from school to back home, and so on and so forth, but let's take a closer look at what sedentarism actually looks like in our modern world.

The shocking truth is that the average person that lives in technocratic or oligarchic countries and continents like the United States, China, Europe, Russia, and most modern "civilized" countries today, in majority of cases, lives a sedentary lifestyle. Let me know if this sounds familiar to you or someone you know; you wake up and do your routine, whether it's have coffee and sit and read, or make breakfast and sit and eat - then you might brush your teeth, shower, and get ready for work or for your day. If you work outside of the home, then you get in a vehicle of some sort, and drive to work. Once you get to work, unless you work in skilled labor like construction, plumbing or something similar, then you work sitting down, or if you're in the small percentage of people who swapped out their chairs for a stand up desks, then you work standing still.

You might get up a few times to go to the bathroom, get some water, take a smoke break or snack break, grab lunch, but most of the time you're sitting or standing in front of a computer screen all day. After work, you drive back home sitting, make some dinner, and sit again, and eat. Most people feel too tired by the end of the day to do any exercise, so they might sit and watch TV, have dinner, and go to sleep.

For a growing vast amount of people around the world, while it might seem like they are busy with all of these day to day tasks, and it feels like you're constantly moving - the reality is, your mind is moving much more than your body. From sitting in the morning, to sitting in the vehicles driving to and from work, to sitting or standing all day at work, to sitting at dinner and watching TV, to laying down• and sleeping - for many people, that means sitting, standing still, or lying down not moving the body in the way it was designed and intended to move, constitutes 90-95% of your life. And while sleep is critical for the function of healing and regenerating the body, that's usually another hours of lying down, not moving, right?

So for the average person, during a 24-hour day, sits, stands, or lies down for about 22 hours out of that 24-hour period. And the other 2 hours is the accumulation of short walks to the bathroom or to and from the car. Does this sound familiar? Like anyone you know?

And if you're someone in skilled labor, you might move a bit more often, but I would venture to bet that majority of people not only in office jobs, or who are retired, or who are in skilled labor, are still not implementing the most effective amount of functional movement as well as the 4 types of medicinal movement that we're going to cover in this chapter.

Why is movement so important for the function of health, healing and rejuvenation? There's many factors why, but here's 9 primary reasons a healthy movement practice is critical to helping you overcome cancer:

1. Improved sleep
2. Reduced pain
3. Increased immunity
4. Natural detoxification
5. Longevity
6. Lowered cancer risk
7. A better quality of life
8. Reduced inflammation
9. Prevents obesity, heart disease, and other chronic diseases
10. More energy, focus and clarity

Now any one of these reasons is a good enough reason to have healthy daily movement practice or routine, but when they are all combined, it's a no-brainer! When you move the body the way it was meant to move, a lot of natural healthy processes occur - including the pumping and flushing of the lymphatic system.

The lymphatic system helps remove waste from the body including bacteria, viruses, toxins and abnormal cells and cancer cells. The lymph nodes house immune cells that help kill off abnormal cells and other harmful substances. The lymphatic system is a major part of the immune system.

But the lymphatic system does not have its own pump like how the blood system has the heart as the pump - the lymphatic system requires stimulation, most commonly through the contraction of muscles and increased heart rate to help pump the fluid throughout the system and remove the toxins and abnormal cells from the body. The lymphatic system needs to be pumped every day to help rid itself of toxins.

If you are not contracting your muscles on a daily basis and getting your heart rate up and breathing heavily doing physical activity, then the lymphatic system is continuously being overloaded by these toxins and by abnormal cells, and can eventually lead to chronic disease like cancer.

Another reason healthy daily movement and exercise is critical is because it supports good liver health. Excess fat in the liver causes inflammation and can lead to less insulin sensitivity, ultimately leading to fatty liver disease, diabetes, and even death. It's been proven that intense exercise like weight training can reduce liver fat and help improve blood sugar control in people who are obese or have diabetes.

The American Heart Association states; *"Science has linked being inactive and sitting too much with higher risk of heart disease, type 2 diabetes, colon and lung cancers, and early death."*

Additionally, exercise supports better sleep, more energy, weight loss, reduced inflammation, reduced pain, and a longer and healthier life. We've all heard that exercise is critical to being healthy, but how often do you actually exercise? The reality is, more and more people are exercising less and less, and it's due to an ever-expanding workforce that lives in front of computers. And, even if you work in skilled labor, like construction, you might be moving more than the average person, but you're unlikely moving the body in all the ways it was meant to move, which can eventually lead to chronic back pain, joint pain and toxic cellular buildup in the body.

I'm reminded of the famous saying, "if you don't use it, you lose it." Here's a great example of what happened to me. Growing up in a small town in Montana, I was always an active kid. My parents had me in sports since I could run. I played soccer, basketball and football since I was old enough to join the teams. During the long cold winters, I skied and snowboarded on the weekends, and nearly every day during the winter breaks.

And when I was around 12 years old I started skateboarding. Skateboarding became a huge passion of mine. Some days I would spend 8 hours a day skating. I was very active; jumping, climbing, running, squatting, falling, moving my body constantly. While some of these sports are also damaging to the body, like getting tackled over and over again playing football, or falling down a hundred times a day on hard pavement skateboarding down handrails, they at least kept me moving.

At school we had P.E., so that was another hour or so each day of movement. Unfortunately, the rest of the day at school we sat all day long, in chairs, which is horrible for the body and leads to chronic back pain and joint problems, but after school I was usually doing something active for at least a few hours.

Then after getting consumed by the fast and toxic life of drugs, alcohol, and partying at a very early age, I knew I had to leave all that behind, change my life, and so I moved to California and started my life over at 18 years old. I got into a corporate job selling phones, and thankfully I was standing on my feet walking back and forth all day long, squatting up and down grabbing phones and accessories from the ankle high cabinets in the kiosk - but that only lasted for about a year and a half before I quit and got into real estate, eventually opening my first business with 7 other partners and then leaving that company to start an advertising business with my spiritual mentor at the time, beginning a physically detrimental 9 year period of sitting at a desk 10-12 hours a day while starting and running my own businesses.

I would try to make time a few days a week to go to the gym, or do yoga, but I could never be consistent with my movement routine. I wasn't motivated enough by just "looking good" to keep up with going to the gym every day, and I didn't yet have a passion for physical fitness as I do today, and I didn't yet have the knowledge about the importance of good movement practices for health and longevity as I do today as well.

I would go to the gym and workout 3-4 days a week, for maybe a month or two, then I would stop going for weeks, even months at a time. I also didn't understand biomechanics, physiology, medicinal movement or therapeutic exercise like I do today. What happened was that I was slowly becoming sedentary, forming poor spinal posture, and creating back pain and joint pain from sitting for too long and not moving enough.

The modern chair, as useful as it might seem, is one of the worst inventions for the physical health of human beings. How the hips and knees are placed at 90° angles, forces the psoas, iliacus, TFL, piriformis and pectineus muscles which are all attached at different areas within the hips, the lower spine and the femur, to either shorten, contract or compress due to abnormal positioning of the body while sitting, while at the same time, the glute muscles get lengthened, creating an imbalance between the various muscle groups, ultimately leading to things like lower back pain, knee pain, and even sciatica. While sitting in chairs might seem like the most "normal" thing we could possibly do, the reality is, it's the most unnatural and unhealthy position for our body to be in.

Many people who live in 3rd world countries actually sit the way we were designed to sit. We are designed to sit cross-legged, in a full deep squat position, or in various seated positions - on the ground. If you watch kids who are outside playing, without any chairs around, you

113

will see how they sit naturally, on the ground, and they constantly move, from one various cross-legged or squatting position, to another. This is exactly what our bodies are designed to do, and it keeps our hips, knees, ankles and back healthy and pain-free for our entire lives.

By sitting in chairs for hours and hours a day, never getting into squatting positions or cross-legged positions on the ground like we're designed to do, it causes all kinds of problems with the body. Many of which we've already discussed, including the ultimate potentiality of cancer and other chronic diseases. This is what happened to me. I started developing chronic low back pain and hip and knee pain due to sitting for too many hours a day.

I couldn't get into a full squat position any longer, I couldn't hold something overheard and squat down like we're designed to do, I couldn't sit cross-legged without chronic pain, and I was only in my late 20's by this point.

And then I found a love for trail running using the pose form running method which actually helps build healthy joints, while focusing on stretching before and after every run, which began to heal my back pain, and eventually found CrossFit and functional fitness, and then began taking back control of my body, focusing on healthy movement 5-6 days a week, stretching, exercising, running, swimming, cycling, weightlifting and gymnastics while also spending 30-60 mins each day doing self-body work, stretching, mobility, qigong and seeing a chiropractor twice a week.

I've now become an athlete in the sport of CrossFit and am enjoying competing with the goals to compete as a professional athlete, when just a few years ago I was headed down the path of long term chronic pain and sedentarism. While I spend more time exercising each day than most people would ever need to because I'm training as an athlete, the reality is, anyone can improve their overall quality of health and physical function by simply implementing the movement principles we ll were designed with, and that's true no matter your age or physical limitations.

I just watched a 90-year-old man lift 405 pounds, two times, and did it like it was nothing! We have a woman in her 70's who couldn't sail anymore, then after coming to our gym and doing CrossFit for a year, she was able to sail again pain free and regain the strength that she lost. We have paralyzed men who come to the gym in wheelchairs, and still find ways to move their bodies and stay active even without the use of their legs - truly remarkable!

And within only a few short years on this new path, my own body has gotten 60-70% of its original range of motion back, 90% of my back pain has been eliminated, I'm much happier, I sleep better, I love exercising now simply for the love of it, and I know I'm on a path for living longer and healthier with less physical complications than ever before.

I still have a way to go, but I am seeing and feeling the improvements over time, and that's the key to success - small, consistent, daily habits that lead to long term progress and results. If you want to live longer, healthier, without chronic disease and with less pain and more physical freedom, then you must exercise and move the body in the ways it was meant to move.

So we know how critical exercise and movement is to our overall health and well-being, but the next important questions are how much movement, how often should we be moving, what forms of movement should we be doing, and what can we be doing each day if we work in front of a computer, or even as a skilled labor person, to improve our body's ability to thrive?

Here is the generally accepted prescription for exercise from cancer.gov for people of all ages, who want to stay healthy, "*The U.S. Department of Health and Human Services Physical Activity Guidelines for Americans, 2nd edition, released in 2018, recommends*

that, for substantial health benefits and to reduce the risk of chronic diseases, including cancer, adults should engage in:

- 150 to 300 minutes of moderate-intensity aerobic activity, 75 to 100 minutes of vigorous aerobic activity, or an equivalent combination of each intensity each week. This physical activity can be done in episodes of any length.

- They say do muscle-strengthening activities at least 2 days a week

- And balance training, in addition to aerobic and muscle-strengthening activity."

So what does this actually mean in a real life scenario? Aerobic activity is anything that gets your heart rate up to 55-85% of your maximum heart rate. So what's the difference between moderate-intensity and vigorous-intensity aerobic exercise?

Moderate-intensity activity includes anything ranging from fast-walking to swimming, cycling, light jogging or even mowing the lawn. An easy gauge for this is that your breathing accelerates to the point where you're breathing at a higher rate than normal, but you can still hold a conversation with someone. For example, if you're jogging at a light pace, and you can still hold a conversation, that's a good indication of light-moderate intensity aerobic capacity.

If you increase your running pace to the point that you can still hold a conversation, but you have to take big breaths every few words, then you're pushing towards vigorous aerobic activity, which has its own healing benefits as well.

The 2nd form of movement is vigorous aerobic activity, which includes all of the same types of movements, such as cycling, running swimming, even kickboxing, dancing and zumba, but at a higher intensity. Vigorous aerobic activity pushes your heart rate closer to that 85% range. The most accurate way to measure your intensity is to get a heart rate monitor and pay attention to it as you exercise. (When diagnosed with cancer, I would recommend avoiding vigorous activity at first as to not overburden your body with biological repair mechanisms. You want majority of your energy to go towards finding and eliminating cancer cells, so avoid this form of exercise until your cancer is in remission, then adding it in will be very beneficial.)

The third form of movement that is recommended for ultimate health and longevity is muscle-strengthening activities (or strength training). Strength training includes lifting weights, powerlifting, gymnastics, bodyweight movements like pushups, pullups, squats, banded workouts, resistance training, heavy gardening or any activity that specifically strengthens the muscles and joints, ideally through compound movements that utilize full range of movements through the joints.

Some great examples of simple and effective compound movements that strengthen the muscles and joints while moving through the full range of motion of the joint are squats that go below parallel, pushups that touch your chest to the floor, and pullups that pull your chest all the way to the bar. If these are new movements for you, then you'd likely need to work on flexibility and strength through modified versions of these movements, while also working on flexibility and mobility to expand your range of motion. Hiring a personal trainer is the first best step in doing strength training safely and effectively.

And the fourth form of movement you should be doing weekly is balance training. Balance training is anything that helps support overall balance and neuromuscular function. Three great examples of this are yoga, tai chi and qigong. Creating and reinforcing your neuromuscular function through balance helps support you through the rest of your physical exercises and supports a healthy brain, healthy joints, and safety through proper movement patterns.

So, adding all this up into a weekly schedule, here's what it should look like for optimum health and healing, (as a cancer prevention model) I call this the Medicinal Movement Routine. To create your ideal routine, fill in the worksheet in the back of this book.

- **Monday, Wednesday, Friday**: 30 minutes of yoga or qigong followed by 30 minutes of light-moderate intensity exercise like swimming, fast walking, light cycling or jogging. You can split this up morning and afternoon or do them back to back.

- **Tuesday and Thursday**: 30 minutes of strength training using bodyweight calisthenics, gymnastics, free weights, weightlifting or powerlifting + 30 minutes of vigorous intensity exercise like faster running, a spin class, cardio kickboxing, faster cycling, or Crossfit. (Most Crossfit classes I've been to are about an hour long and include both strength training and vigorous intensity exercise. But before doing any Crossfit classes I highly suggest hiring a personal trainer who can help you achieve greater flexibility, balance, safety and strength before you dive headfirst into Crossfit. A good Crossfit coach will help you be safe, but not all coaches are the same, so take your time making sure you find someone who understands your current physical limitations as well as your goals and can help you create a path towards slow but steady progress through safety and proper movement)

- **Saturday**: 30 minutes of yoga or qigong followed by 60 minutes of light-moderate exercise like jogging, cycling or swimming - again you can split these up or do them back to back.

- **Sunday**: Rest

To make it easy, make sure to fill in the worksheet in the back of this book so you can follow it each week.

Of course this sample schedule is not perfect for everyone, and not one size fits all, but this is a great example of what you can and ideally should be doing each week based on the recommendations provided by The U.S. Department of Health and Human Services Physical Activity Guidelines. If you're currently not exercising, or doing less than 50% of the sample schedule, then I suggest increasing your total exercise volume by about 10 minutes each week until you are at the minimum suggested volume as outlined above.

If you go from no exercise, or very little exercise, to lots of exercise too quickly, you could get injured. So the best thing to do is start small. You can start walking 15-20 minutes per day if you have not been exercising at all, and it will reap huge rewards over time. You can also hire a personal trainer, let them know your ideal goals and your current limitations, and have them assist you in slowly but steadily progressing to the suggested amount of volume over the next 3-6 months until you are comfortably-challenged with the amount of exercise suggested.

If you get to a point where you feel you are ready to go above the minimum suggested amount of exercise each week, and you are moving safely and effectively, and you're feeling like you need more to achieve better results, then set your sights on a goal in the future like running a 5k race, swimming a half mile or full mile, or cycling a digital race at home (yes you can do those with applications like Zwift, you don't even have to go on the dangerous stress if you don't want to) Or even lifting a certain weight and breaking your own personal records.

In addition to this suggested schedule, there are simple, but effective daily movements you can do throughout the day while you're working at your desk. These little things that I do while working at the computer help me stay focused, increase lymphatic function, improve flexibility, reduce pain, and improve overall health and wellbeing.

You can watch the bonus video I've made as part of this book called Simple Daily Movement Practices and go through this simple practice together with me. If I have long days at the computer, I will do a variation of this at least 3-4 times a day, though I usually do a full workout in the morning and another one in the evening as well, but this is a great way to stay moving throughout the day and support you on your healing journey.

You can access this video inside the Health and Healing Club at www.HealthAndHealingClub.com

Before we go any further, I understand some of this might be overwhelming, and some of this you might already know, but right now is a great opportunity to take a self-assessment and recognize how often you are actually moving your body as suggested in the sample schedule.

Are you exercising doing moderate to vigorous intensity movements (cardio) 5-6 days per week for at least 30-60 minutes each day? Are you doing balancing activities like qigong and yoga 3 days a week for at least 30 minutes each day?

Are you doing strength training at least two days per week? If not, please be honest with yourself, and also recognize that if you want to prevent and even try to reverse cancer - or at the very least - live longer, healthier and happier with less pain, less chronic disease, and more vitality and youthfulness - then you need to make a commitment right now to hiring a personal trainer, getting yourself to the gym or just having a simple space in your house where you can have a few pieces of basic equipment like rubber bands and dumbbells, and creating a progressive schedule that gets you to these minimum numbers.

It might be challenging at first. It might be uncomfortable. It might feel weird or embarrassing - especially if you haven't exercised like this for years, decades, or even ever! But I promise you, the more consistent you are, the more dedicated you are, and the more you stay focused and fully committed to the process - you will see progress, you will feel etter, you will start to enjoy it, and you will get healthier. It's not a ope or a dream, it's a science and reality. It's how we were designed. Ve were designed to move every day, and when we move in this way ur brains release endorphins, dopamine and serotonin, rewarding you or doing what you were designed to do. And after a few weeks, you'll tart looking forward to it, and after a few months, you'll feel like ou're starting to love it, and after a few years, you'll feel like a brand ew person!

Another place you can access bodyweight, more gentle movement outines is inside the Health and Healing Club. I have personally ecorded exercise routines for all levels of fitness, including if you are verweight or have trouble moving - and you can access those classes nside HealthAndHealingClub.com - there's an entire routine program a their called Healing Back Pain, and it's a great bodyweight novement series of videos that you can do at home. You can access hat entire program inside the Health and Healing Club.

To complete this section, here's the most important thing to consider out a daily movement practice. It needs to be something you enjoy. you enjoy it, you'll stick to it. All exercise feels hard and umbersome at first, but the more you do it, the better you'll feel, and ie more often you'll stay on track.

Ask yourself these questions: What's your deeper reason why you ant to heal cancer? Is it to live longer? To fulfill your life's purpose? o be a better parent or grandparent? To enjoy the remaining years of our life with more energy, happiness and vitality? To leave a legacy? o contribute to society in some way? Whatever your deeper reasons hy, remind yourself of them every day when you step into that gym, turn on that exercise video, or take that qigong class.

Remind yourself of your deeper reasons for committing to the ocess. Remind yourself that even when it's challenging, it's going to lp you live longer, healthier and with more purpose in your life. mind yourself that a daily fitness routine is going to help you achieve

121

your goals in life, enjoy more of your life with less pain, and experience more health and happiness for years to come.

Find something you enjoy. Try new things. Try tennis or racquetball. Go get swimming lessons. Start fast walking, then jogging. Try martial arts. Put on your favorite music, go to the gym and try cycling. Hire a personal trainer and have them teach you the in and outs of lifting weights safely and effectively. Take a zumba class, try dancing, start golfing, get a trainer, and stay committed to the process.

Once you find something you love, that helps you move every single day, you will look forward to it, and it won't be a chore, it will be blessing. That's the key to sustained fitness - it needs to become lifestyle, and it needs to be something you enjoy and look forward to, so if you've tried a few things and nothing's stuck with you yet, try new things until something sticks. There's something for everyone, an once you find it, you'll know, and it will consume you in such a good way it will add years to your life and life to your years!

Now that you've got a foundation for your daily movement routine it's time to put it all together, create your personalized blueprint into what I call a holistic plan of health and healing, and make it last.

That's what the 7th and final step is all about.

If you've made it this far, give yourself a huge pat on the back, you've accomplished more already than 90% of people ever will. You're committed to this process so I'm committed to you. I'm here to truly help and serve, and I'll keep giving and giving because I know it's for people like you who will go all the way and give it everything you have to be the best and healthiest version of yourself.

This next and final step is crucial. It's the packaging that wraps all together so you have a daily, weekly, monthly and yearly plan attack, and a strong support system to help you achieve your goals and live life at a higher level of health and vitality.

Step 7. Make It Last, A Holistic Plan for Health and Healing

Wow this is exciting; you've made it to chapter 8 of this 7-step system. And this is the last step of the entire book! This is it! You made it! One final step, and this step wraps everything we've learned together into a daily action plan so you can follow it, modify it, and make it your own!

Over the past 7 chapters we've covered everything from learning how to accept and even appreciate the fact that not only are we all going to die, and how to not let death be a deterrent from living our best lives, but how we are all here to truly live, and live with health and vitality!

We've covered the 3 top principles for taking back your power, and how to activate your own inner healing capacity. I shared with you the blueprint, questions and principles for building your integrative success team.

We've explored the sympathetic nervous system in depth and I shared with you the importance as well as practical strategies for keeping your sympathetic response turned on as often as possible so your body activates it's inner healing capacity more often than not.

I gave you the 12 major cancer causing culprits and how to immediately and effectively remove them from your life. Then we went into depth about how to nourish and rejuvenate your body using the most scientifically proven nutrition and lifestyle choices.

Finally, in the last chapter, we explored the science of movement and I gave you the 4 proven pillars of what I call Medicinal Movement.

At this point, having gone through all 7 chapters before this, you have such a strong foundation, a set of principles, and more importantly strategic action steps you can take every day moving forward to help your body heal.

And this next step helps bring it all together!

And please note, as I've said before, there's no single blueprint or magical cure that can guarantee a cure for cancer, not even the best oncologists or pharmaceutical companies can say that, especially with a 98% failure rate with chemotherapy as we explored in depth in previous chapters. But there are principles and foundations, along with methods and strategies, that are proven elements for helping the body do what it is designed to do, heal itself! And that's exactly what we covered in this book.

If for some reason you missed any of the previous chapters, it is imperative that you go back through them, before you complete this step. Step 7 is the combination and personalization of all of the important information and strategies we covered throughout all of the previous chapters.

Without knowing the information, we covered in the previous chapters, this step will only partially serve you - All 7 chapters' prior are a prerequisite to fully benefit from the value of this final step.

So now it's time to make it your own. I've designed a simple pdf printout called the Holistic plan for health and healing. Why Health and Healing? Why not just health, or why not just healing? Because even though they are interlinked, they are actually two different states of being.

Healing is the process, health is the outcome. The reality is, we are always either healing, and moving towards health, or we are deteriorating, and moving towards disease. Health is a destination, but it's like following a rainbow, you can move toward the rainbow every day, and even one day you might find yourself right next to the rainbow, but if you stop moving, that rainbow disappears.

So we have to look at healing as the constant process by which our everyday actions are helping us achieve. And we look at health as the ultimate goal for which when we are healthy, then our lifestyles continue supporting healing, so we never go back towards disease. Make sense?

To put it another way, let's say you follow all of the principles and strategies we've covered in this book, and with the help of a little bit of grace, you're able to reverse cancer. You reach a state of health. But then, you decide to go back to your old lifestyle, eating cheeseburgers and smoking cigarettes and sitting around not moving enough - then disease is most certainly going to come back, and then you have to start all over again with the process of healing, which as we know, takes time.

Versus, if you continue with the lifestyle that has helped you heal, then you will constantly stay in a more balanced and harmonious state of healing and health, and it will be much easier to stay healthy and vital, without sliding backwards. Ok? So that's the goal, help you live healthier and more vital and transform your lifestyle so you can enjoy more years ahead.

Right now I want you to fill in the worksheet in the back of this book, titled, Holistic Plan for Health and Healing, and I want you to stick to it, ok? Remember the 3 principles for taking back your power?

Become your own healer, be patient, and never give up. This is the time to truly implement those principles into your action plan.

And once it's filled out, it's done. You might decide to modify it as you go, or your integrative success team might encourage you to modify certain aspects of it for your own personal journey - which is great! Just remember to stick to the foundations and the principles.

Additionally, if you tear it out and make blank copies of it, then you'll always have a blank version of this plan, so if you need to change it from time to time, just print out a new one, modify it, and stick it on your fridge, and then follow through. You've made it this far, you owe it to yourself to at least give yourself 1 year on this action plan. If you don't see any improvements in one year, then it's time to change it up, but I can promise you that by following this action plan fully, you will be in a much better position to be able to add years to your life and life to your years - and who knows, maybe, just maybe, you'll reverse cancer and help inspire others in the process.

So that's it. It's done, it's ready to go! Congratulations, you have a holistic road map for supporting you on your healing journey for months and years to come. And remember, it's important to track results and modify as needed every 6 months or so.

And now that we've finished going through your holistic health and healing plan, join me in the final chapter for some closing thoughts as we wrap up our time together. This last chapter is very short, but please join me as I share my gratitude, my final wishes for you and share with you some additional next steps.

Chapter 9

Closing and Next Steps

I just want to say, as we close out our time together, that I'm truly grateful and honored for your trust in me, and your trust in this process, and I don't take it lightly. I know your time is valuable, and I truly value your time and the time we've spent together.

I hope this is the beginning of a long and meaningful relationship, and truly wish you the most success in your journey ahead.

I just want to remind you that health and healing is a process. It's a lifestyle. And it's a way of being, a way of thinking, and a way of living.

Nothing worthwhile happens overnight, and even though the path we've laid out together is simple, it's not always easy. So giving yourself the flexibility for change and adaptation, and giving yourself the patience and compassion is critical in your process forward.

My goal is that you come to find, as Chris Wark, Elaine Gibson, and Dr. V all have found through their cancer journeys, that cancer is a wakeup call, and it's a blessing. It brought them some deeper awareness about themselves. It brought them closer to their spiritual essence. They turned it into a calling to help others. And I hope that it will bring you a deeper sense of purpose and meaning in your life. No matter how scary it might be, because underneath the surface there's always gold worth finding. There's always sunshine after rain. Blue skies after a stormy night. And as we tap into our deeper calling to help others through our own struggles, we tap into the deeper essence of what makes us human.

And that's truly the most fulfilling thing in life, right? Being able to contribute to others in a meaningful way. Whether it's through education or through service. Whether it's through helping support someone through a challenging time or sharing with them some useful tool, service or informational resource like this one that can help change someone's life for the better.

The more you come in tune with your inner-calling, the more you focus on your own growth as well as contribution to others, the more fulfilled you'll be in the remaining years of your life, no matter how short or how long.

We both know that we're all going to die someday, right? But the question is, did we truly live? Did we make the world better in some way? Did we contribute positively to other people, animals, or the planet? And if the answer is yes, then let's keep doing it! And if the answer is no, then you've still got work to do!

And I want you to know that I'm here to support you for months and years to come. That's why I hope you'll join the Health and Healing Club, if you haven't already, because inside the members area you'll get ongoing support from world renowned experts and cancer survivors sharing with you more resources and strategies for living your healthiest life yet. You'll get to ask ongoing questions to diverse and trustworthy experts, and you'll have access to the same insider-information that I have access to. So please go do that right now, setup your account at www.HealthAndHealingClub.com and I'd be honored to have this resource contribute towards your healing journey.

And please let me know about your progress over the coming weeks, months and years. I want to hear your updates, I want to know your challenges, I want to celebrate your successes, I want to share your story with others to inspire others to live their healthiest and most fulfilled lives.

Together we can contribute to a healthier, happy, and sustainable world. And please tell others about this book. Please help me get this life-changing information out to those who need it. You can share the link BecomingCancerFree.com with anyone you know who has cancer and who is ready for walking down the path of healing. Together we can make a difference in more people's lives around the world who need our help.

And that's my dream, to create sustainable health-centric communities around the world that live in harmony with the planet and each other, teaching, learning, growing and contributing together towards a healthier and regenerative world. So I hope you'll join me in that dream and join me in staying committed to this life of health, happiness and vitality.

Again, thank you, I'm truly honored for you taking the time to commit to this process, and I can't wait to hear about your progress in the coming months! I wish you all the love, health and healing in the world. Be well!

With love and appreciation,

Nathan Crane

MY INTEGRATIVE SUCCESS TEAM

4 Key Traits

Questions to Ask

1. Diversity
2. Expertise
3. Specificity
4. Collaborativity

3 Key Areas

1. Functional, Integrative, or Holistic Medical Doctor (MD)
2. Naturopathic Doctor (ND) or Doctor of Oriental Medicine (MOD)
3. Emotional Healing / Spiritual Healing Expert

1. Have you successfully helped anyone else with my stage of disease reverse it completely?
2. What were the key areas that you focused on that helped that person reverse the disease?
3. How long did it take?
4. What are your main areas of focus and expertise as a professional?
5. What kind of support and treatments can you help me with even if I can't come to your clinic in person?
6. I am building my integrative success team, and I'm looking for experts who are willing and open to collaborate with other experts, of course following all the HIPAA laws, but to

131

**For access to dozens of world leading experts who fit these key traits and areas join the Health and Healing Club at:

HealthandHealingClub.com

share information, data and reports with one another based on my personal request, and work together to not only help me find my best healing path, but to help all of us learn and grow in the process? In short, are you willing to collaborate with other experts that I bring onto my team?

7. What kind of cost am I looking at long term working with you? What financial options do you have? Do you take insurance? What forms of insurance do you take and what do they cover?

8. Do you have an option where I can call you at any time if I'm having an emergency, or need an expert to talk me through an important decision?

9. If we started working together today, what are the first steps you would have me go through?

CANCER CAUSING CULPRITS

Timeline

1. I will remove 80% of these from my life by:

   _____ / _____ / _____

2. I will remove the remaining 20% of these toxins from my life by:

   _____ / _____ / _____

Cancer Causing Culprits to Remove

- Plastics. All plastic cups, bowls, and water bottles - anything plastic that you put liquid into.
- Bedding. All non-natural, non-organic, polyester or other processed material bedding including pillows sheets and blankets, must go.
- Body care products that have chemicals, preservatives and dyes.
- Animal products. Remove all meat and dairy from your diet.
- Stop buying processed food. All dried and packaged foods like cookies, crackers, chips, pasta, ice cream and pizzas, with preservatives or chemicals.
- Reduce sugar exponentially. Only eat whole plant foods

that have their natural healthy sugars intact.

- Stop drinking processed drinks and alcohol.
- Reduce EMF exposure. Turn off phone and Wi-Fi router at night.
- Reduce pollution exposure. Add 1 plant per 100sqft to your home.
- Remove pollutants from your water. Use oxygenated and filtered water.
- All chemical-based, fire-retardant, carpets and rugs should eventually be replaced with natural woods, not chemical woods, or organic non-chemical carpets.

MEDICINAL MOVEMENT ROUTINE

Hiring a Trainer

Start with a trainer twice a week to help you learn how to move safely, then build up from there.

Find Your Joy

Find something you enjoy. Try new things. Try tennis or racquetball. Go get swimming lessons. Start fast walking, then jogging. Try martial arts. Put on your favorite music, go to the gym, and try cycling. Hire a personal trainer and have them teach you the ins and outs of lifting weights safely and effectively. Take a zumba class, try dancing, start golfing, try Crossfit,

Medicinal Movement (Sample Schedule)

(Based on the U.S. Department of Health and Human Services Physical Activity Guidelines for Americans, 2nd edition) Here is a sample scheduled I've designed.

Monday, Wednesday, Friday: 30 minutes of yoga or qigong followed by 30 minutes of light-moderate intensity exercise like swimming, fast walking, light cycling or jogging. You can split this up morning and afternoon or do them back to back.

Tuesday and Thursday: 30 minutes of strength training using bodyweight calisthenics, gymnastics, free weights, weightlifting or powerlifting + 30 minutes of vigorous intensity get a coach, and stay committed to the process.

exercise like faster running, a spin class, cardio

kickboxing, faster cycling, or CrossFit.

Saturday: 30 minutes of yoga or qigong followed by 60 minutes of light-moderate exercise like jogging, cycling or swimming - again you can split these up or do them back to back.

Sunday: Rest

HOLISTIC PLAN FOR HEALTH AND HEALING

My Healing Goals

1.

2.

3.

Taking Back My Power

Daily Affirmations

1. I am becoming my own healer, I am responsible for my health
2. I will be patient, I know true healing takes time, knowledge, and action
3. I will never give up, I will persevere until I heal, learning, improving, and growing up as I go

Mindset

Inner peace is an absolutely essential part of my healing journey. Healing my body is only one portion of the process, healing my mind and emotions is just as important. I am committed to my healing

My Integrative Success Team

My Integrative, Functional, or Holistic (MD):

My Naturopathic Doctor (ND):

process. I know it can take time, and I know nothing is guaranteed, but I will stay focused and committed to the journey

My Emotional Healing Expert:

7 CORE SLEEP PRINCIPLES

My New Sleep Routine	**Sleep Principles**

My New Sleep Routine

In Bed by:

_____

Awake at:

_____

Electronics off at:

_____

Hours of Sleep:

_____

Sleep Principles

- All electronics off 1 hour before bed. This is the minimum amount of time, though 2 hours is ideal. Why? Because the blue light from the screens, and the content coming from the electronics stimulates the brain and prevents melatonin from secreting properly. So, 2 hours if you're really dedicated, but 1 hours is the absolute minimum.
- Replace all light bulbs in the house with blue light blocking lights. This is a game changer. And it's based on the same reason as #1 - the blue light from the bulbs causes your brain to stay awake, reducing the production of melatonin, affecting your quality of sleep
- Get black out curtains in your room, put all electronics in airplane mode, unplug the wifi router, and make sure you have no lights, no matter how small, whatsoever in your room at

night when sleeping. Lights from the moon and stars are actually very healthy for your brain, but lights from the streets, neighbors electronics, including EMFs from wifi, can disrupt your natural circadian rhythm, causing less sleep efficiency. So that means clocks, phones, and all electronics turned completely off, so there are 0 lights and 0 EMF stimulation while sleeping.

- No caffeine 8 hours before bed. This one is huge. If you want to be asleep at 10pm, then no caffeine after 2pm. Even if you think caffeine doesn't affect your sleep because you fall asleep easily even after a cup of coffee, think again. When you start measuring your quality of sleep, you'll find that caffeine inhibits your body's ability to enter Deep Sleep efficiently, and once you stop having caffeine 8 hours before bed, because that's how long caffeine takes to get out of the system, you'll see your sleep quality drastically improves.

- Follow a daily routine. For the most beneficial sleep quality, and for the harmonizing of your circadian rhythm, it has been scientifically proven that the best quality of sleep for adults is between the hours of 10pm-2am. This is when the deepest and most regenerative sleep happens. If you are missing any of those hours of sleep starting at 10pm, you're missing out on some of your best deep sleep benefits. Additionally, having a routine, where you go to bed and wake up every morning at the same time, and you do it with the same habits such as, brush teeth, use the bathroom, read a book, meditate, fall asleep. And you wake up at the same time every day, your circadian rhythm is optimized and your sleep is deeply enriched.

- Do not eat at least 2 hours before bed. Ideally, your body should not be digesting food while you sleep. It should be using that energy on healing and cellular repair. The more time you give your body to digest, before you go to sleep, the more your body can repair damaged cells, including cancer cells, while you sleep. And this is one of the reasons why intermittent fasting, giving your body at least 14 hours of non-eating time each day, so from stopping eating at 8pm, and not eating again until 10am, will give you incredible healing benefits that help reduce inflammation and fight off cancer cells

- Get 8 hours or more every night. According to the extensive sleep research I've done, 8 hours is truly the minimum any adult should get each night if they truly want to heal. But if you're really far along in cancer, the more sleep the better. If you can get 9 or 10 hours, even better. If you can take a 1-2 hour nap during the afternoon, even better. The more sleep you get, and the better quality of sleep you get, the faster you will heal - there's 0 debate about that among the scientific community. Many of us were raised being told don't be lazy, get out of bed, don't sleep all day! And while that might have been the norm growing up, the reality is, you need to do the opposite of that advice if you want to heal

About the Author

Nathan Crane is a natural health researcher and holistic cancer coach. He is an award-winning author, inspirational speaker, Amazon #1 bestselling and 20x award-winning documentary filmmaker.

Nathan is the Director of the Health and Healing Club, President of the Holistic Leadership Council, Producer of the Conquering Cancer Summit, Host of the Conquering Cancer Documentary Series, and Director and Producer of the award winning documentary film, Cancer; The Integrative Perspective.

In 2005, at only 18 years old, Nathan began his health, healing and spiritual journey, eventually overcoming a decade of brutal teenage addiction, house arrest, jail and challenging times of homelessness to become an international author, filmmaker, researcher and educator.

Nathan has received numerous awards including the Accolade 2020 Outstanding Achievement Humanitarian Award, and the Outstanding Community Service Award from the California Senate for his work in education and empowerment with natural and integrative methods for healing cancer.

With more than 15 years in the health and wellness field as a researcher and advocate, Nathan has reached millions of people around the world with his inspiring messages of hope and healing.

Receive a Free Download of his eBook, 5 Natural Pillars for Preventing and Reversing Cancer at: www.NathanCrane.com

Printed in Great Britain
by Amazon

80480154R00088